HINDUISM

FOR SCHOOLS

Seeta Lakhani

Edited by Jay Lakhani

Vivekananda Centre London Ltd
6 Lea Gardens Wembley Middlesex HA9 7SE
http://www.vivekananda.co.uk

Key stages 1,2,3	Hinduism for Schools site: http://www.hinduism.fsnet.co.uk
Teachers Guide Notes	Specially prepared GCSE Hinduism guide notes can be obtained by emailing us at hindu@btinternet.com
ICT	Links to various websites on Hinduism can be accessed through Vivekananda Centre Site: http://www.vivekananda.co.uk/schools.htm

ACKNOWLEDGEMENTS

Images

The authors and publishers thank the following for permission to reproduce copyright images and photographs in this book: Himalayan Academy & Hinduism Today, Kapaa, Hawaii for many of the images. BAPS Swaminarayan Sanstha London, for images of Diwali and Holi. Hubblesite.org for the image of a double star cluster. Geeta Thakerar, Vinoobhai Wadher and Kamal Persaud and Bhavit Mehta, for allowing us access to their collections of images. Bharatiya Vidya Bhavan for the photos of Bharatnatyam and Bhajan recital. Atul Shah for the image of Mahavir Swami and the Ramakrishna Order for all images and quotes of Sri Ramakrishna and Swami Vivekananda et al.

Every effort has been made to contact the holders of copyright material but if any have been inadvertently overlooked, the publishers will be pleased to make the necessary alterations at the first opportunity.

Note:
The word 'man' has been used in this book in its most generic sense.
Frequent use of terms like: 'Divinity of man', 'Relationship between man and God, the 'Role of mankind' etc., should not be interpreted as promoting a gender bias.

ISBN Number 0-9549567-0-2

First published in 2005 by: -
Vivekananda Centre London Ltd

Cover Design by
Sister Gayatriprana

Designed & Printed in Singapore by Graphic's Zone

Contents:

This book is dedicated to

Sri Ramakrishna

Author's Thanks

I feel honoured to be given the opportunity of writing this book. I am tremendously grateful to my father for creating the basis and structure of the GCSE notes, for his rigorous editing and for providing many new and exciting perceptions on various aspects of the Hindu religion. I appreciate his help in writing chapter six on the philosophy of religion and chapter ten on science and religion. Without him, this book would not have been possible.

I am very grateful to the Himalayan Academy, Hawaii, for readily supplying many of the images and artwork for this book. Their beautiful artwork and photography brings Hinduism to life and I am very thankful for the magazine's support. I am also extremely grateful to Elsie Mack for her tremendous patience and support in proof reading and editing. Her meticulousness ensured greater clarity in the presentation of many subtle aspects of Hinduism in this book. I would like to thank Sister Gayatriprana for producing a beautiful front and back cover design for this book and am very grateful to Dr. S. Buddheo and Ashok Chabria for their moral and financial support. It is thanks to Vikas Thakrar that the GCSE Hinduism material of the Vivekananda Centre London was placed on the web, where a structured set of notes has benefited many people sitting the Hinduism examinations. I am very grateful to Arun Chabria, Dilip Ladwa and Rajen Shah for helping with the formatting of the book.

Seeta Lakhani

Preface

Though this book is primarily written for use by schools teaching Hinduism, it can also be used by lay readers looking for a structured understanding of this subject. Each chapter is divided into the 'main text', 'breadth of vision' and a 'memory guide'. The 'breadth of vision' incorporates material that offers deeper insights into Hinduism.

The two most serious challenges faced by world religions today are: First, in a world that has become a global village, to find a way that religious communities can coexist peacefully and with full dignity. Secondly, to make religions relevant in a modern, secular society. Hinduism has important contributions to offer in both these areas. In response to the first of these challenges, this book develops the theme of 'religious pluralism' in detail. The second challenge faced by the world religions is the struggle, taking place at a deeper level. It is the struggle between religious and non-religious worldviews. What "9/11" revealed is not a conflict between two world religions but a conflict between religious and non-religious worldviews in the guise of a 'hard-line' religion fighting a 'materialistic Western world'. The way to resolve this challenge is to subject all religious teachings to the acid test of rationality. Why religions are not expected to abide by the standard of reason, no one knows.

The new discoveries at the cutting edge of modern science are very exciting and are beginning to reveal a spiritual dimension to hard sciences. Some of these discoveries are like the distant echoes of the Hindu philosophy. Werner Heisenberg, the founding father of modern physics, has commented that: One cannot always distinguish between the statements made by Eastern metaphysics and the pronouncements of modern physics. This book (and the next one in the series *Advanced Hinduism*) explores these links.

The source of our authority and inspiration for presenting Hinduism comes from Swami Vivekananda (1863-1902). The late Professor Ninian Smart paid tribute to Vivekananda by saying that it is with Vivekananda that Hinduism as an 'all-India religion' came into being. The most comprehensive and comprehensible face of Hinduism becomes visible through the lectures delivered by him. A unique feature of Hinduism is that it places equal, if not greater, emphasis on contemporary exponents of Hinduism, like Vivekananda. Most texts on Hinduism continue to present the historic rather than the contemporary expression of religion. The fixation some Western authors have on the teachings of *Manu* for example, reflect their own idiosyncratic approach. Hinduism prides itself as being a 'living religion', constantly evolving and refreshing the message of spirituality through contemporary spiritual giants. This book is a contemporary version of Hinduism in contrast to what have now become the antiquated forms.

So far, the portrayal of Hinduism in the West has been *extremely* poor. The special features of Hinduism, such as the 'divinity of man', 'pluralism', 'rationality and religion', or the 'links between science and religion', rarely get a mention. Most books portray Hinduism as a cultural phenomenon: *just a way of life'* incorporating *hereditary caste, many gods and goddesses, idolatry, sati, Kali,* etc. This book is a robust attempt to dispel such poor portrayals of Hinduism, a religion that has a crucial role to play in reviving and refreshing the message of spirituality throughout the modern world.

Jay Lakhani (Editor)
Vivekananda Centre London

Chapter 1
BACKGROUND

Coming to terms with the laws that govern everything ~ that is *Hinduism*

Hindus call their religion *Sanatana Dharma. Sanatana* means eternal & universal. *Dharma* means 'that which holds together'.

Sanatana Dharma

Sanatana Dharma is that which holds society and civilisation together through righteous living. In broader terms it is defined as coming to terms with the eternal laws that govern everything. Searching for and harnessing these laws for the benefit of all is the way to practise religion.

Is this a science or a religion? The definition of Hinduism sounds more like an all-inclusive science than a religion, for example there is no reference to God. This is not a coincidence. There is a close link between Hinduism and sciences; we explore this in later chapters.

Sindhu to **Hindu**

Many world religions are named after the prophets who founded them in ancient times. Christianity is named after Christ; Buddhism is named after Buddha, but the word Hindu is not derived from the name of any particular prophet. The word *Hindu* is in fact derived from the name of a river situated in Northwest India called the *Sindhu*. The word *sindhu* in the Sanskrit language means 'a vast expanse of water'. In a way this word is apt for describing Hinduism, as like the *Sindhu* it is *vast* and *versatile*.

Hinduism
Vast & versatile like the *Sindhu*

Is Hinduism just a way of life?

Many people say that Hinduism is *just a way of life*. This is actually a very demeaning comment, implying that Hinduism is a social or cultural phenomenon rather than a structured religion. A proper study of Hinduism reveals a very mature and well thought out religion. When some Hindus casually comment that *Hinduism is a way of life* what they actually mean is that Hindu teachings have influenced every aspect of their daily lives.

No founders? Or too many founders to count?

For many religions, there is a single founding figure whose spiritual experiences form the basis of that faith. Hinduism does not rely solely on the spiritual experiences of one or two ancient founders but is established on the spiritual experiences of *hundreds* of spiritually enlightened individuals who have refreshed the message of spirituality throughout the ages. Many such spiritual personalities chose to remain anonymous and hide behind a common generic name like *Vyasa*, a *Sanskrit* word meaning 'a compiler', to allow their teachings to merge smoothly with earlier teachings. Hinduism has in fact far too many founders to count.

Hinduism ~ the most ancient *and* the most modern religion

The ability of Hinduism to refresh the message of spirituality through modern proponents allows the Hindu religion to evolve within dynamic social frameworks and contexts over time. The common title given to these founders of Hinduism is *rishi* (the word is derived from the Sanskrit *'drish'* meaning 'to see') which refers to those men and women who claim first hand experience of God. *Rishis* can be young or old, male or female, ancient or modern; they are the true source of authority in Hinduism.

An ancient *rishi*
A *Rishi* is one who experiences God

A Modern great *rishi*
Ramana Maharshi (1879-1950)

Religion is not an invention but a discovery by mankind

The teachings of Hinduism are referred to as *apurusheya,* meaning they are 'not personality based'. Some scholars have misinterpreted this term and translated it to imply that 'Hinduism has no founders'. What this term actually means is that the Hindu religion is not based on personalities but on *principles*. This is a very crucial statement, as it emphasises that Hinduism is a discovery and not an invention of any individual or group of individuals. Just as scientists do not invent the laws of nature but discover them, these founders, or *rishis* of the Hindu religion do not invent spiritual laws but discover them.

Many religions that are personality based, risk losing credibility if it is shown that these personalities are not historic figures or that the stories ascribed to their lives could not have happened.

Personalities classified

Though Hinduism is founded on principles, it also places great emphasis on the personalities who discover and bring these principles to life. These personalities can be classified, as illustrated in the following story:

A story to illustrate how to classify religious personalities:
Four friends walking in a forest, discovered a high, circular wall behind which appeared to be a lot of joviality and music. The four friends were curious to see what was behind the wall. Three of the friends hoisted one of them up to the top of the wall to find out what was happening. This friend was so overwhelmed that he could not tell his friends what he had seen. He simply climbed over the wall and disappeared on the other side. A second friend was hoisted up to the top of the wall. He too, became so excited by what he saw that he started singing and dancing on top of the wall and after some time disappeared over the other side. The remaining two friends were still anxious to look over the wall. The third friend was hoisted up to the top of the wall. He too was overwhelmed with what he saw. He did not disappear behind the wall but straddled the wall and helped the fourth friend up to the top so that he too could see on the other side.

This story symbolically reflects the disposition of different types of spiritual personalities. The first friend, who silently disappeared over the other side of the wall, symbolises those quiet 'seers and sages' who, after become God-realised, inconspicuously merge into God. The second friend who made a song and dance after seeing over the wall stands for those saintly figures who declare their vision of God to others, but are unable to pass on their experiences. The third friend who straddled the wall and helped the last friend to climb up the wall symbolises an *avatar,* an incarnation of God. This third friend is very unique, as he seems to have the power to offer God experience to others. Some Hindus would claim that such personalities are none other than God himself incarnating as a human being.

God descends to earth ~ *Avatars*

The word *avatar* means 'one who descends'. Hindus say that God literally descends to earth for the benefit of mankind and to rejuvenate spirituality. Hindus refer to eminent personalities such as *Rama* and *Krishna* as *avatars*. *Buddha* and *Christ* would also be classed as *avatars*. These personalities are exceptional among saints and seers, as they possess the unique ability to spiritually transform others even with a touch or a look.

***Buddha* as an avatar**
taught that to be good and to do good is religion

Spiritual guides ~ *Swamis & Gurus*

Swami or 'master' signifies mastery over the senses, and is a title customarily used to address monks. *Swamis* traditionally wear ochre coloured clothing, which bears a symbolic connotation with fire, suggesting that *swamis* are individuals who have burnt away their worldly desires. They spend their lives striving for God realisation and for the benefit of mankind. Renunciation is a central teaching in Hinduism, as exemplified in *Krishna's* explanation in the sacred scripture called the *Bhagavad Gita*: "True knowledge teaches renunciation from all attachment." B.G.13.8-12

Guru means a spiritual teacher. The Sanskrit root *gu* refers to ignorance and *ru* implies 'a remover of', hence this word defines the role of the *guru*, as one who removes ignorance.

Acharya literally means a special teacher who instructs through example. *Acharya* is also a title reserved for the head of some Hindu sectarian movements.

The Method of imparting knowledge

Religious teachings are imparted mainly through scriptural studies and discourses. The student is expected to show a great deal of respect for his teacher. The injunctions for the student are *pranam:* respect, *prashna:* enquiry, and *seva:* dedicated service to his teacher. Wholehearted devotion to a teacher is advocated as the easiest method of gaining spiritual knowledge. The student must serve his teacher and deepen his own knowledge through sincere inquiry.

A *Guru*
A spiritual teacher with his disciples

Hindu Symbols

From *Prati* we derive ~ *Pratik* & *Pratima*
The *Sanskrit* word *prati* means 'going towards'. From *prati* are derived the words:
- *Pratik,* meaning a 'symbol' that leads to God and
- *Pratima,* meaning an 'image' that leads to God. (*Murti* is the same as *pratima*)

Hindus make wide use of such symbols and images to lead them to God. Some people criticise Hindus as being **'idolaters'**, or worshippers of images. Hindus are not apologetic about using symbols and imagery; they insist that as long as we operate in a finite world, we all need finite tools to relate to the infinite God. It just cannot be otherwise. Every religion does this; some, like Hinduism, do it knowingly while other religions do it unknowingly. Sacredness ascribed to a cross, a crescent or an ark or a Kaaba or a scripture is unconscious idolatry.

Om
In the beginning was the word and this
word can be heard in meditation

Om
When attaining God realisation through deep meditation, the sound *Om* is heard naturally, hence it is considered to be the most fitting symbol to represent God. Hindus claim that the universe was created out of a reverberation which is given out by the *Om* sound.

Lotus
A symbol of purity and detachment

Lotus
The lotus is frequently seen in Hindu images and stands as a symbol of purity. Though the lotus grows in muddy water it still emerges pure and beautiful. The lotus flower is also symbolic of detachment; just as water runs off the lotus without wetting it, the individual is expected to remain detached from worldliness.

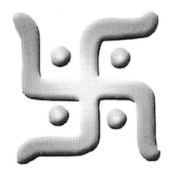

Swastika
May good things come to us from all
four corners of the world

Swastika

The *swastika* symbol (from *swasti* in *Sanskrit* meaning well-being) denotes auspiciousness. The four arms of the *swastika* are there to draw good luck from all 'four-corners' of the world. The symbol is seen at the entrance of temples and Hindu homes, and is frequently used during religious ceremonies.

ॐ भूर्भुवः स्वः
तत्सवितुर्वरेण्यं
भर्गो देवस्य धीमहि
धियो योनः प्रचोदयात् ।

The Gayatri
The central prayer of Hindus asking for God vision

Hindu Prayer

Prayer is defined as the expression of the innermost desires of the heart. Some prayers may ask for good health or wealth, but the prayer that asks for God vision is considered to be the most potent. One such prayer in the Hindu tradition is called the *Gayatri.*

The Gayatri reads: *"Let us meditate on the glorious effulgence of that Supreme Being who has created the universe. May She enlighten our hearts and direct our understanding." (Rg. Veda 3.62.10)* Note: the *Gayatri* refers to God as a *She.*

Breadth of vision

Sanatana Dharma
Both the Sanskrit words *sanatana* and *dharma* bear several layers of meaning that reveal a more comprehensive approach to the idea of religion. The word *sanatana* can mean eternal as well as universal. The Sanskrit root, *dhar* in *dharma,* implies sustenance. The inference is that *dharma* is the principle that sustains everything from the universe to society and civilisation. *Dharma* in a social context, is defined as the cohesive force that unifies society, and the practice of *dharma* becomes 'a mode of righteous living.' However, the most comprehensive definition of the word *dharma* is 'discovering and living by the laws that govern everything external as well as internal'.

Science and Hinduism
The practice of *dharma* as searching for and harnessing the laws that govern the universe is in line with the broad objectives of material sciences. The difference lies in the fact that religions have focused on discovering and harnessing the laws that govern the inner man, the laws that dictate his mind, his emotions and intellect. Hinduism suggests that the theory of everything (TOE) that science seeks will only be achieved if science becomes more inclusive and incorporates the contribution of the innate structure of the mind and the intellect in its worldview.

Social Science and Religion
Hinduism strongly refutes the view that religions are conscious or unconscious inventions of society. Religious truths are discoveries and not inventions, just like any other discoveries of science. Hindus resist the idea that religions are social or psychological ploys employed by mankind. This theme is developed in the next volume in this series.

Prophets
Hinduism recognises the validity of the teachings of the prophets of other religions. It also recognises the 'contextual nature' of the teachings of every prophet. Every prophet has to take into consideration the nature and needs of the society he is dealing with, and present his teachings in a way that is most suited to address these needs. The 'contextual element' in his teachings is recognised as a necessary compromise. No prescription of any religion, including Hinduism, is viewed as 'absolute'. This also means that the teachings imparted by the contemporary prophets are considered more relevant to modern needs. Hinduism places equal if not greater emphasis on contemporary figureheads of religion than the ancient ones.

Symbols
Every symbol used to represent God is a necessary compromise. How can something defined as 'absolute' be expressed through any name or form or through scribbles in any book? All symbols are seen as limited, but necessary tools for focusing our minds on something that is essentially transcendent ~ God.

Memory guide

Sindhu	A vast expanse of water; the former name of a river in Northwest India
Dharma	Searching for and harnessing the laws that govern the universe both external and internal for the betterment of mankind
Rishi	One who sees God; a generic name given to the founders of Hinduism
Apurusheya	Not man-made; refers to spiritual teachings that are based on principles rather than personalities
Avatar	One who descends; the name given to a God-man who has the capacity of infusing spirituality in society
Swami	A person who has mastered himself. A monk
Guru	A spiritual teacher who helps remove the ignorance of the student
Acharya	A spiritual teacher who practises what he preaches
Pranam	To fold the hands and offer salutation
Seva	Dedicated service
Prashna	Use enquiry for spiritual progress
Om	A sound heard in the deepest of meditation; the key Hindu symbol
Lotus	A flower symbolic of detachment and purity
Swastika	A symbol invoking auspiciousness and good luck from all directions
Gayatri	The central prayer of the Hindus, praying for God vision

EXTRA NOTES:

Chapter 2
CONCEPT OF GOD

Pluralism is not Polytheism
One of the greatest misconceptions about Hinduism is that it is viewed as a polytheistic religion (meaning belief in many almighty Gods) or that it is a henotheistic religion (promoting a hierarchy of Gods). Both these claims are incorrect. The best way to classify Hinduism is to call it a **pluralistic** religion. Pluralism is a uniquely Hindu idea. It suggests that every one of us relates to God in a different way. As we are all different, individually or as groups, the way we relate to God has to be *necessarily* different. This is not a statement of compromise but a statement of fact. The concept and approach to God that we adopt has to reflect our inclinations including our social and historic backgrounds; it cannot be otherwise.

To gain a better understanding of pluralism let us ask ourselves: "Why should God be thought of only as our father in heaven, why not as our mother in heaven?" We can then take this questioning further and ask, "Why should God be thought of only as a personality (male or female) and not as a principle that underlies everything?" Some of the brightest minds in modern times prefer this second approach as it does away with the idea of God as a personality. In their opinion God as a personality introduces too many unanswered questions.

Denominations are a *grudging* acceptance of pluralism
The fact that every religion has a large number of denominations is a *grudging* acceptance of religious pluralism within that faith. This variation should be accommodated with dignity by embracing the idea of pluralism. Pluralism is already inherent in all world religions. Advocating religious pluralism is the best way of avoiding friction between different sectarian movements within a religion and between different religions.

Celebrating many ways to God is an inherent feature of Hinduism
Pluralism opens up a plethora of perceptions and approaches to God in Hinduism. These approaches are classified into three broad groups:

Three Main approaches to God

God:	viewed as a **personality** with attributes and *form*
	viewed as a **personality** with attributes but *no form*
	viewed as a **principle** that underlies everything

1. God as a personality with attributes and form ~ *Saguna & Sakara*
God with attributes, *saguna,* and form, *sakara,* is the most popular approach adopted by Hindus. The corporeality attributed to God allows the devotee to develop a relationship with the Ultimate Reality (God) viewed as a personality, and is therefore considered to be the simplest way of relating to God. This personified God can be regarded as kith and kin, for example as a father or mother, a brother or sister, or maybe a child or a friend. There are a vast number of relationships that the devotee can choose from in order to build a relationship with God. This is not seen as a limitation but as a very practical way of relating to and approaching God.

Man is not made in the image of God ~ God is made in the image of man

As we are human it is easy to relate to God as a *super* human. Thus we portray God in our image. The depiction of God in human form has to incorporate superhuman attributes. This is traditionally done through the portrayal of a deity with many arms or heads.

'Higher beings' ~ *devas* are not God

The misunderstanding that Hinduism is polytheist religion may have arisen from the literature of Hinduism, that talks of 'higher beings', called *devas* and *devis* (meaning the 'shining ones' who live in other astral planes). These two words often get loosely translated as 'Gods' and 'Goddesses', creating the appearance of a multitude of Gods and Goddesses in the Hindu religion.

Infinite power must include the power to become finite

Abrahamic religions (i.e. Christianity, Judaism and Islam) promote the idea of God with attributes such as omnipotence (all-powerful) and omniscience (all knowing), but resist giving a form to God. These religions insist that the infinite God cannot become finite. Hindus disagree; they say that having infinite power must include the power to become finite. They claim that the gracious God assumes a finite form for the devotee who loves him. The form He assumes is imposed by His devotee. This is the reason why we find many images of Gods and Goddesses in the Hindu tradition. This is a celebration of pluralism and should not be confused with polytheism.

Religious Pluralism
Same God thought of differently as *Shiva*, *Vishnu* or the Mother Goddess

The Same God fulfilling different roles ~ *Trimurti*

The same God fulfilling three different roles is called *Trimurti*, 'three in one'. God depicted as three in the forms of *Brahma*, *Vishnu* and *Shiva*.

Brahma is God playing the role of the *creator* of the universe, and is shown with four heads pointing in four directions. He has four arms and holds a rosary and the scriptures. He is shown seated on a lotus; his vehicle is a goose.

Vishnu is God in the role of the *preserver* of the universe. In two of his hands he holds the divine weapons, a mace and a discus. He also carries a lotus and a conch shell. The vehicle of *Vishnu* is the eagle. *Vishnu* is sometimes shown reclining on the coils of a giant snake.

Shiva is God (sometimes) depicted in the role of the *destroyer* of the universe. The *Shiva* devotee would strongly disagree with this singular classification. *Shiva* for them is the creator, preserver and destroyer. *Shiva* is customarily shown in two postures. The first is called *Yogi-raja* and shows *Shiva* in a meditative pose, smeared with ashes symbolic of renunciation. A snake curled round his neck represents his perfection in meditation and the river *Ganges* flows from his hair. *Shiva* is shown with a third eye on his forehead, which symbolises that he is spiritually awakened.

The second posture of *Shiva* is called *Nataraja* or Lord of the dance. *Shiva* in this pose engages in the dance of both *creation and destruction*. He holds the drum as a symbol of creation, and fire, representing destruction. He dances on a dwarf figure, which symbolises ignorance. *Shiva* is shown offering protection and boons to his devotees with his other two hands.

Vishnu
The Gracious God who takes on human forms to help mankind

Nataraja
Shiva engaged in the dance of creation and destruction

The same one God fulfilling different roles

Shakti
God as female

Cosmic Power is feminine: *Shakti*

The idea of viewing God as a female is very popular with many Hindus. The Ultimate Reality as female is called *Shakti*, which means power. It is believed that the energy driving the universe should be viewed as female. The essential nature of every physical object in the universe is energy, *Shakti*. Thus worshipping God as a female, is an acknowledgement of the fact that the cosmic power is viewed as feminine. Some renowned forms of 'God as a Mother' are *Parvati*, *Durga, Kali, Lakshmi* and *Saraswati*.

Shiva and ***Parvati***
God and his manifesting power are inseparable

Durga
Invoking strength to overcome adversities

Parvati is the consort of *Shiva*. Though depicted as an ordinary woman, she is considered to be the personification of cosmic power, *Shakti*.

Durga is seen in the role of the destroyer of evil; shown holding many divine weapons, and seated on a lion or a tiger, symbolic of the suppression of the ego.

Lakshmi
Beauty personified as a Goddess

Saraswati
The Personification of intelligence

Lakshmi the consort of *Vishnu*, is the goddess of wealth and beauty. She is often shown wearing a red sari, seated on a lotus and holding lotuses in her hands. She is shown bestowing blessings and offering gold coins to her devotees. The English word 'lucky' is likely to have originated from the Hindu word *Lakshmi.*

Saraswati is the consort of *Brahma* and is the personification of knowledge and aesthetics, expressed through art, music and dance. She is therefore traditionally shown playing the *veena,* an ancient stringed instrument, and wearing a white sari as a symbol of purity. *Saraswati* holds scriptures in one hand, symbolic of knowledge and a rosary in another, symbolic of austerity.

Kali is female force in the role of the all-destroyer, hence she is shown in a fierce form. The word *kali* is derived from *kala,* which means 'time' - the all destroyer. She is depicted with black skin and streaming black hair, wearing a necklace of skulls. Her terrifying appearance suggests that God is not only the creative force, but also the destructive force of nature. Hinduism says that if we accept that God is the creator of the universe, then we have to also accept that God alone has the power to destroy it. *Kali* is the fierce form of God that ends one cycle of creation in order to start a new one.

Eminent *avatars: Rama, Krishna & Buddha*

Vishnu in the role of the preserver of the universe takes on human forms called the *avatars.* He descends to the world for the destruction of evil and the benefit of mankind. One scripture says that He descends to earth ten times. Some *avatars* are given greater prominence and are worshipped as God by many Hindus. The most popular being *Rama*, the seventh *avatar*, *Krishna*, the eighth *avatar*, and *Buddha* the ninth *avatar*.

Rama is considered to be the ideal man, *Purushotama*. He is the best example of how an ideal son, ideal father, ideal king should behave and is depicted as the hero of the epic the *Ramayana*. He lived for principles and not for possession; it is difficult to find any other king, ancient or modern, who has lived up to such high moral ideals. His consort *Sita* is recognised as the personification of loyalty, grace and chastity and is revered as the ideal woman by Hindus. *Rama* is shown with blue skin, carrying a bow, and is accompanied by his wife *Sita* and his faithful devotee *Hanuman*.

Krishna is regarded by his devotees to be the perfect *avatar.* He is the author of the sacred Hindu scripture, the *Bhagavad Gita.* He is shown with a peacock feather in his hair and carrying a flute. His consort is *Radha;* the love they share is not physical but the spiritual love that draws all souls to God.

Buddha is regarded as the ninth *avatar* of Vishnu. He lived in the sixth century BC. The word *buddha* means 'one who is enlightened' and the religion he taught is called Buddhism. It teaches that 'to be good and to do good' is the central teaching of all religions.It is a religion that focuses on the issue of suffering and how to eliminate it. Buddha is normally shown seated in meditation wearing white or yellow clothes.

Rama & Sita
The ideal man & ideal woman

Radha & Krishna
Idealised love between the Soul and God

Popular figures of Hindu worship ~
Hanuman & Ganesh

Hanuman is the embodiment of strength and intelligence, and is depicted as the dedicated servant of *Rama* in the epic *Ramayana*. He is shown with a monkey-face, carrying a mace and a mountain, signifying strength. *Hanuman* is considered the best role model for Hindu youth, as he personifies strength, intelligence and a celibate lifestyle.

Ganesh is the son of *Shiva* and *Parvati.* He is the remover of obstacles and the patron of good luck. He is shown with an elephant-head. *Ganesh* represents auspiciousness and is propitiated when initiating any endeavour, such as business, travel, or marriage.

Animals or birds shown with various deities
Because some of these deities are shown with animal faces, it does not mean that Hindus worship animals or promote animal behaviour. The reason why these animals are shown with the deities is to promote the idea of the sacredness of all living things. Hindus disagree with the teachings of some religions that God has made animals and birds *purely* for the consumption of mankind. Hindus go along with the theory of evolution that we are a continuation of the animal kingdom and this reverence for life should be extended to the animal kingdom.

Rama and *Sita* with **Hanuman**
Hanuman is the personification of strength and celibacy

Nandi
Shiva's vehicle

Ganesh
Removes obstacles and brings good luck

2. An attributive God but without form ~ *Saguna & Nirakara*

Some Hindus prefer to think of God with attributes (*saguna*) like 'love', 'truth, or 'power', but just as in the *Abrahamic* traditions, God is not given any form or shape (*nirakara*). Two recent Hindu movements called the *Arya Samaj* (Society of Nobles) founded by *Dayananda Saraswati* (1824-1883) and the *Brahmo Samaj* founded by *Ram Mohan Roy* (1772-1833) advocated this approach. Both these movements brought about important reforms in the ritualistic practices and also prompted many social reforms. As most Hindus prefer to think of God with form *as well as* attributes, these two movements failed to generate greater popular support.

The *Havan* Ceremony

The *havan* ceremoy is the traditional *Vedic* worship through fire. This ceremony is called *havan*. A fire is lit in a special pyramid shaped vessel called a *havan kund*. Clarified butter called *ghee*, and nine types of grains are offered to *Agni,* the God of fire, as a means of building relationship with higher beings. The sacrifice of *ghee* and grains is a symbolic gesture of sacrificing the ego. This ritual is performed at many religious ceremonies like weddings.

Havan
Fire ceremony promoting the idea of self-sacrifice to make spiritual progress

How can God be both with and without form?

A metaphor used by a recent Hindu prophet called Sri Ramakrishna (1836-1886) explains how the same God can simultaneously be both *with* and *without* form. The example he gives is of ice and water: Both ice and water are essentially the same, but one has form and the other is formless. In the same way, he says, "God can be both with and without form. It is the love of the devotee that freezes the formless God into the form the devotee chooses. Many are the names of God and infinite the forms through which He may be approached. In whatever name and form you worship Him, through that you will realise Him".

Ice and water
Same thing *with* and *without* form

3. God beyond all classifications ~ *Nirguna & Nirakara*

The third approach to God in Hinduism is to think of God as formless, *nirakara,* as well as without attribute, *nirguna.* This may appear very abstract and difficult, and yet this approach provides the best link between science and religion. This approach takes pluralism to the other extreme. It moves dramatically away from the idea of God as a personality, to the idea of God as a principle. The idea that God has a particular form or that he has superhuman attributes like omniscience or omnipotence is seen as human limitations imposed on the concept of God. As we are human, the only way we can relate to God is in human terms, and thus we give him various human forms and superhuman attributes like being 'all compassionate'. Some people recognise the limitations of such approaches and thus prefer to adopt this third approach. The word 'God' is now replaced with the term 'Ultimate' or 'Cosmic Reality' *Brahman.*

Vivekananda has emphasised the importance of moving away from the idea of God as a personality to the idea of God as the principle that underpins everything. Modern thinking man will find it easier to relate to spirituality if this *third* approach to God is promoted.

Vivekananda (1863-1902)
The comprehensive proponent of modern Hinduism

Brahman
That which manifests as everything. The whole cosmos is a projection of that principle

God as a cosmic principle ~ *Brahman*

This third approach to God in Hinduism requires us to think of Him or Her not as a personality (with attributes like love and power), but as a principle underlying absolutely everything. This principle forms the basis of everything we experience. *Brahman* is the Ultimate Reality *appearing* as everything. It manifests as all the galaxies, all the living and non-living things, and even as our mental and intellectual faculties. Everything is seen as an expression of this Ultimate Reality, *Brahman*. This approach is similar to the one used by scientists who are also trying to find a unity from which everything is manufactured. To pay tribute to this idea, Hindus define the universe as *shrishti*, meaning, 'projection' of *Brahman*.

Note: Hindus do not say that the universe is God; that theory is called **pantheism**. Instead they say that God or the Ultimate Reality appears or manifests as the universe. In this manifested universe, living beings are considered to be more special than non-living things. *Brahman* becomes more manifested in living beings. This gives rise to the second key concept in Hinduism: *Atman*.

Supreme dignity offered to mankind ~ *Atman*

Hindus say that we *are* all essentially God. This is a dramatic statement. No religion has given such dignity to mankind. We are being equated to God! Many people are frightened off by such ideas. They ask, "We do not feel like God, we certainly do not behave like God so how can we be God?" Hindus say that the reason is because we have never tried to discover our true Self. We get attached to what *we think* we are rather than what *we truly are*. We associate ourselves with our bodies and minds and not with the essential thing that is looking out through our minds and bodies. That essential thing is God. To illustrate this point let us make use of a metaphor.

One God looking out through all these eyes: Imagine going to the seaside on a sunny day. On the peak of every wave we see the sparkle of the sun. It appears as if the sea has come alive with thousands of suns sparkling on the surface of the water. In the same way, say Hindus, the same one God sparkles as *consciousness* in the eyes of every living thing. The conclusion of the Hindu philosophy is that 'It is God alone who manifests himself as the universe (defined as *Brahman*), and finds clearer expression as *consciousness* in all living things (defined as *Atman*).' Our essential nature is God. The sole aim of religion is to discover this spiritual fact. This Hindu idea offers supreme dignity to mankind, and also offers the best reason why all living things should be respected and why we must help each other. God, according to this belief, is not somewhere 'out there' in the heavens, but is really our own true Self. By beginning the journey of self-discovery, we end up by discovering God. According to this finding, the highest worship of God is 'service to mankind and respect for all living things.' It is the same God who percolates through nature and appears most transparently in all of us. This is the Hindu version of Humanism: it is called ***Spiritual Humanism.***

Atman
Just as the crest of every wave reflects the same one Sun,
it is God alone who sparkles as consciousness in the eyes of every living being

The Relationship between *Atman* and *Brahman*

Brahman is defined as the Ultimate Reality (God) appearing as everything including all living things. *Atman* is defined as the *Ultimate* Reality (God) appearing as our essential Self. Simple logic suggests that there cannot be two *Ultimate* Realities else we have a contradiction in terms. How can there be two Ultimates? Hence we are forced to conclude that *Atman* is the same as *Brahman*, quoted in the Hindu scripture: *'Aham Brahmasmi'* (*Brihadaranyaka Upanishad.* 1.4.10). Some Hindus dislike the idea of equating ourselves with God as it sounds arrogant, hence they modify the relationship. They say that *Brahman* (God) is like the fire and the individuals (*Atman*) are like the sparks of that same fire.

So which of the three Hindu approaches is best?

The answer is: "The approach that suits our temperament and needs is the best approach for us." Many in the Hindu tradition prefer to think of God as a personality like *Shiva* or *Vishnu* or the Mother Goddess, as it is easier to relate to them and build a loving relationship with them. Some Hindus prefer to think of God as their essential Self (*Atman*), and some Hindus who are perhaps more scientifically oriented prefer to think of God as the essential nature of everything (*Brahman*). The approach that suits us is the best for us. No one particular approach is considered to be better than any other approach. As we are all different, the way we approach God will necessarily be different. As Sri Ramakrishna states, "As many individual opinions, that many paths to God".

Sri Ramakrishna (1836-1886)
The Prophet of Interfaith who claims the same God experience through
Islam, Christianity and Hinduism

Hinduism ~ A family of sectarian movements

Under the umbrella of Hinduism a vast number of very diverse sectarian movements exist side by side. Sometimes this can cause confusion, but this is accepted as a price paid for pluralism. Every approach to God, from the crudest to the most sophisticated, has a place in Hinduism. Just as in any democracy we find vastly contrasting ideas given room for expression, Hinduism makes space for vastly differing approaches in spirituality. Hindu sectarian bodies exist side by side with each other with full dignity and without compromise. Some of the better known sectarian movements are:

- *Vaishnavites* - those who worship *Vishnu* as the supreme Godhead. They can be devotees of Vishnu, or of *avatars* of *Vishnu* like *Rama* or *Krishna*. These include the *Swaminarayan, Pushtimarg & Iskcon* movements.
- *Shaivites* - those who worship *Shiva* as the supreme Godhead.
- *Shaktas* - those who worship God as the female power. They may be devotees of any of the forms of the Mother Goddess like *Parvati, Durga, Kali* etc.
- *Arya Samaj* - A movement set up by *Dayananda Saraswati* promoting the idea of a formless God.

Two contemporary sectarian movements that stand out for making a very positive contribution to the promotion and portrayal of *comprehensive* Hinduism in the West are:

- The *Vaishanvite* movements operating as the *Swaminarayan Sampradaya* &
- The *Shaivite* movement operating as the *Himalayan Academy*

Satguru Sivaya Subramuniyaswami
The founder of Himalayan Academy

HDH Pramukh Swami Maharaj
The spiritual head of BAPS
Swaminarayan Sanstha

"My Religion is Best"

The idea of pluralism offers the best prescription to how people of different religions can co-exist with full dignity. Pluralism teaches that all religions are different pathways to the same God. How to translate this teaching of pluralism into practise can best be illustrated through a story.

Story illustrating how to practise religious pluralism:

Two young boys were playing in the school ground. One boasted, "My mum is the best in the world." The other objected strongly and said that his mum was the best in the world. Both the boys loved their mothers and were not prepared to accept the other's statement. Soon they came to blows. A wise man, passing by, enquired why they were fighting. Both the boys declared passionately that their mother was the best, and hence the other was wrong. The wise man told both the boys, "Take my advice: feel free to declare passionately 'my mum is best' but then add two little words at the end of the sentence. Say, 'my mum is best... *for me*'. You will then find that there is no disagreement or cause for quarrel." The two boys readily agreed and became friends.

The moral of this story is that it is fine to declare that our religion is best, but we must add the two little words at the end: our religion is best *for us*. This idea needs to be incorporated by all the major world religions, especially those that claim exclusivity. Some world religions claim that theirs is the only true pathway to God, whilst all others are erroneous. This is bound to create a lot of strife and conflict in the name of religion. The resolution of this serious global issue lies in the pluralistic teaching of Hinduism. *All* religions are *true* and *valid* pathways to God. 'My mum is best *for me*', becomes 'Our religion is best *for us*, but not necessarily for the rest of mankind'.

Pluralism allows many religions to co-exist with dignity

Rationalists have always argued with the exclusivist world religions like Christianity and Islam that if they both claim to contain an almighty God then they have contradicted each other. How can there be two almighty Gods? Richard Dawkins, the famous biologist was put off religions at an early age by such exclusivist claims. The resolution can only come if these religions abandon exclusivist claims and incorporate pluralism by saying, "We just reflect one point of view about God, there can be many others." Pluralism allows diversity within and between religions, it even makes an attempt to reconcile these differences. It promotes community cohesion by dispelling the myth that any one religious body holds a monopoly on God

Conversion ~ pressurising people to *shift* from one religion to another

As Hinduism is based on pluralism, conversion from one religion to another is viewed as unnecessary and counter-productive. Hinduism does not advocate that a Christian should become a Hindu, neither does it advocate that a Hindu should become a Christian. (See chapter 10)

Learn to 'accept' other religions: Hinduism disagrees with comments like, 'We must learn to tolerate other religions' as this is a patronising statement. Hinduism teaches that we must not only *tolerate* other religions but we must be able to *accept* other religions as valid. So then it is foolish to expect people to convert from one religion to another. Methods of conversion carried out in the past, and even at present, show many religions in a very poor light. Most conversions took place through sheer force; they were carried out at the point of a sword or a gun. Some conversions took place through fraud and fear by suggesting that if a person does not convert he is destined to go to hell to be tortured for eternity. Some conversions took place through financial inducement (bribery) or through imposition of financial penalties. As any rational person can appreciate, none of these methods show religions in a good light. Even in a modern enlightened world, such obnoxious practices continue and become the source of animosity and friction between religious communities. However, it must be stated that the teaching of pluralism does not insist that a person cannot change his religion if he feels a *natural* urge to do so.

Religious Pluralism
Plural ways to the same Ultimate

Pluralism also implies that we can choose our own way to find God:
Pluralism in practice means exercising a choice of ways to reach God. The path one adopts depends on one's own temperament. Four major pathways or *margas* have been advocated in Hinduism. The individual can choose a pathway, or a combination of pathways, most suited to his personal needs. These pathways are sometimes referred to as the four *yogas*. The word *yoga* means 'union', suggesting that these pathways lead to union with God.

Four pathways to God

Bhakti	Karma
Jnana	Raja yoga

1. The pathway is also the goal ~ *bhakti yoga*

Bhakti yoga is the way to God through devotion and love. Those individuals who are emotionally inclined and feel naturally drawn to God prefer this method. *Bhaktas* or devotees spend time in prayer, worship and constant remembrance of the deity they are attracted to. They attempt to gain first hand vision of God and engage in activities such as scriptural reading, devotional singing, telling beads and associating with other devotees. By carrying out such activities with great devotion and love, these individuals develop closer relationship with God, culminating in God vision.

Sri Sarada Devi, a saint of modern India stated that, "As one gets the fragrance of a flower by handling it, in the same way one gets spiritual awakening by constantly thinking of God." The resulting intense love for God is the means as well as the end. 'Intense love' is both the pathway and the destination, hence *bhakti yoga* is considered by many as the sweetest pathway to God.

The majority of Hindus aspire to be true *bhaktas*, devotees of God. However the problem lies in the fact that it is extremely difficult to maintain such intense love for God. Some devotees worship God so that they can receive some benefit, like wealth, in return. This is not recognised as supreme devotion, as the relationship forged is transactional. True *bhakti* or devotion is desire for God alone, love for the sake of love. The devotee desires nothing from God but God himself. This exceptional kind of love for God is only acquired by a few and is termed *parabhakti* or supreme devotion. *Chaitanya*, a seventeenth century Hindu saint, observed that "devotion to God clears the mirror of the mind". Examples of *parabhaktas* in the recent past are *Meera, Tulsidas, Tukaram* and *Ramdas*. *Ramdas* observed, "when God is victorious in your heart, all darkness born of ego-sense disappears. There is then nothing but a feast of immortal joy and peace for you".

Bhakti
The Path of devotion is the *sweetest* way to God

Meera
A recent Hindu saint who followed the path of devotion to gain vision of *Krishna*

2. The Path of action: Detachment in the midst of activity ~ *karma yoga*

Karma yoga is the path of action, suited to those who are active by nature and love to work. *Krishna* in the *Bhagavad Gita* teaches that 'action is better than inaction'. Action is unavoidable; even if the body is still, the mind continues to conjure up thoughts and be active. The aim is not to stop acting, but to act in a way that will purify the mind. Therefore the individual must continue to act but he must act with the correct attitude. All activities should be selfless. This like the other paths, ensure that a transition is made from an ego-centred living to a God-centred living. The *karma yogi*, the ego-less actor, therefore fulfils his duties devoid of pride, culminating in a sense of detachment in the midst of activity. This process of non-attachment eventuates in identification with our real Self, the *Atman*, which is the witness and not part of what is being witnessed. *Mahatma Gandhi* said "I am endeavouring to see God through service to humanity, for I know that God is neither in heaven nor down below, but in everyone." *Karma yogis* must learn to live for others rather than for themselves in order to attain enlightenment. Vivekananda, who was instrumental in bringing Hindu teachings to the West, is one of the best examples of a recent *karma yogi*.

Karma
Selfless work leads one to God

3. The path of wisdom ~ *jnana yoga*

Jnana yoga is recognised as the means to God through the sheer force of reason. Followers of this pathway aspire to reach God by purifying their vision of reality through sharp intellect. Through this process, the individual sees the world in a different light. A similar progression is happening in science; our worldview today is dramatically different from that of ancient man.

The key tools required by *jnanis* or spiritual intellectuals, are dispassion, *vairagya,* and discrimination, *viveka*. Dispassion is a key requirement for such individuals, who develop a strong sense of detachment from the world by controlling their desires. Discrimination means constant reviewing of what is real and permanent, in contrast to what is unreal and temporary. This allows the individual to see the world in a different light. Practitioners of this path reason: "This is not ultimate reality, neither is that", *neti neti*, until what is left can no longer be negated. A few examples of individuals who have successfully attained enlightenment through this path are *Shankara* (788-820), *Vivekananda* (1863-1902) and *Ramana Maharshi* (1879-1950).

Ramana Maharshi ascertained that "for the ignorant, the self is defined by the body; the wise know that within the body the unlimited Self shines with its own splendour".

Ramana Maharshi
Focused insight reveals God

4. Experiential religion through the path of meditation ~ *raja yoga*

Raja yoga is often confused with *hatha yoga,* which focuses on physical postures and exercises; however *raja yoga* is the path to God through meditation. The first requirement to succeed in meditation is for the individual to have a healthy body, hence physical exercise or *hatha yoga,* was introduced. Having a healthy body is only the start; next, one has to learn to sit motionless for long periods of time in order to bring the mind under control. *Raja yoga* means 'royal path' suggesting that this is the 'royal pathway to God'. This pathway is suited to those who are contemplative by nature. It is advocated as a practical experiment to find God and was codified by *Sage Patanjali* around the eighth century BC. The practice he prescribed consists of eight steps that allow the individual to gain mastery over his mind and body. This practice involves the development of one-pointed concentration called *dhyana*, culminating in enlightenment or union with God called *samadhi.*

Sage Patanjali's teachings about *yoga* form one of the major schools of Hindu philosophy (See Chapter 3). Despite its centrality within Hinduism, *raja yoga* is a difficult path to follow due to the severe disciplines it demands.

Meditation
God has to be experienced

Vivekananda in London 1896
God experience is not confined to prophets who lived in ancient times

No path is better than any other ~ you choose a pathway that suits you or create a new one
It is important to recognise that all these four pathways: *bhakti, jnana, karma* and *raja yoga*, all eventually lead to the same God experience. It is foolish to think that one pathway is better than any other. Most individuals will choose a combination of pathways that suit their temperament, or may create their own special pathway to God.

Breadth of vision

The Hindu idea of Pluralism
- Does not suggest that the ultimate is plural (that is a contradiction in terms) but that there are many (plural) ways to conceive and approach the ultimate
- Pluralism is not a new religion which incorporates appropriate bits of all religions ~ that idea is viewed as a grotesque caricature of all religions
- Pluralism is not *'relativism'* which suggests that there is no Absolute, hence almost 'anything goes'. This teaching insists that the Christians follows the Christian prescription to the letter, it insists that the Hindus follows the Hindu prescription to the letter. Though the prescriptions are *necessarily* different they are strictly *binding.*
- Pluralism does not require anyone to water down his faith to accommodate other faiths but requires one to dig deeper into one's own faith to discover the validity of other faiths
- The world religions no longer have the luxury of *just* existing side by side with each other; out of sheer necessity they now have to reconcile their worldviews

Reference to Pluralism in the Hindu Scriptures of authority
"There is only one Reality, different sages call it by different names." (*'Ekam sat vipra bahudha vadanti' R.V. 1.164.46).* Some may see the ultimate reality as a father in heaven others may want to see it as a mother in heaven whilst others would prefer not to view it as a personality but as a principle that underlies everything. All these different views are considered valid; they reflect our own limitations and approaches to spirituality.

Consequences of Pluralism
The maturity of Hinduism is manifested in the way it celebrates and promotes pluralism. It teaches that the same God (or ultimate reality) has been thought of and promoted in various ways by different prophets of different religions to suit the needs of the people they were interacting with. Hence every religion will necessarily be different and yet there is an underlying unity behind all such approaches.

Reconciling religion with science
Pluralism offers dignity and validity to differing religious approaches to spirituality. But then if spirituality is such a universal phenomenon it cannot be restricted to mere religious expression. Hinduism suggests that every focused human endeavour should reveal a spiritual edge. Hard sciences too, are discovering spirituality through the process of searching for unity in diversity. This theme is developed in the next textbook in this series.

Searching for the common ground in religions
One of the major philosophical challenges faced by world religions is the question: "If there is only one God, how can there be more than one exclusivist religion? Many monotheist religions claim exclusivity on God, so either one of them is right and the rest are wrong, or more likely, all are wrong. In philosophical language, this is termed as 'playing one religion against another.' The resolution to this issue is in the pluralistic teaching of Hinduism. The concept of God, instead of being a dividing force, becomes a unifying force sustaining all religions.

All religions are 'different'
Different religions are seen as different approaches adopted by different God-men for promoting spirituality in different historic and geographic frameworks. As such, every religion is contextual. The theme it wants to promote may be universal but the manner in which it is portrayed and translated into practice has to relate to the people it is dealing with, and as such, has to be 'relative' and not 'absolute.' It is very important that this idea is appreciated and incorporated by world religions, as it grants validity and dignity to every approach in spirituality.

Memory guide

Pluralism	The view that there is a multitude of ways to think of and approach spirituality (based on personality or principle)
Saguna & Sakara	God viewed as a personality with form and attributes
Saguna & Nirakara	God viewed as formless but with attributes (e.g. love)
Nirguna & Nirakara	God viewed as a principle and termed as Ultimate Reality that underpins everything
Atman	Ultimate Reality manifesting as Self consciousness
Brahman	Ultimate Reality manifesting as absolutely everything
Trimurti	God viewed as fulfilling three different roles: *Brahma* the creator, *Vishnu* the preserver, *Shiva* the destroyer
Nataraja	'Lord of the dance'; *Shiva* in cosmic dance of creation and destruction
Shakti	God viewed as female, the driving force of the universe; *Parvati* consort of Shiva; *Durga,* destroyer of evil; *Kali,* destroyer of the whole creation; *Lakshmi,* giver of wealth & beauty; *Saraswati,* patron of arts, music, dance and knowledge.
Rama	*Purushotama,* the ideal *avatar,* the ideal man
Krishna	The perfect *avatar,* author of the *Bhagavad Gita*
Hanuman	The embodiment of intelligence and strength, the monkey-faced deity who helped *Rama* defeat the demon *Ravana*
Ganesh	Harbinger of good luck. The elephant-headed deity, who removes all obstacles
Havan	The worship through fire; fire is used as a messenger to higher beings and God
Margas	Different pathways to God
Yoga	Seeking union with God
Bhakti Yoga	The way to God through intense devotion and love; God for the sake of God alone is called *parabhakti,* supreme love
Jnana Yoga	The means to God through sharp intellect, using the tools of discrimination and dispassion
Karma Yoga	The path of action; purify the mind through selfless acts
Raja Yoga	Meditational discipline as a means to enlightenment

EXTRA NOTES:

Chapter 3
SCRIPTURES

Principal and subsidiary scriptures

Hindu scriptures are divided into two broad groups: the principal scriptures called the *shrutis* and the subsidiary scriptures called the *smritis. Shruti* scriptures focus on the spiritual experiences of the 'seers' called *rishis,* whereas *smriti* scriptures present the narrative aspects of religious teachings. The *smriti* scriptures include the historic, mythological, social, ethical and philosophic texts of Hinduism.

Scriptures of supremacy ~ the *Shrutis*

The Sanskrit word *shruti* translates as 'that which is heard', implying that this knowledge was 'heard' or experienced by the *rishis* in deep meditation. Another reason why these scriptures may have been called *shrutis* is that they were originally conveyed orally over hundreds of years. It was only much later that these teachings were actually written down. These are the authoritative texts of Hinduism and they contain the essence of God experience. Some portions of the *shrutis* are often recited during worship ceremonies, at special religious events and during rites of passage.

Scriptures
Written records of God experience (*Vedas*) are
the spiritual treasures of mankind

Invocation, ritual and philosophy ~ contained in the four *Vedas*

The *shruti* texts are called the *Vedas*. This term derives from the Sanskrit root *vid* meaning 'to know' hence simply put *Vedas* are books of knowledge. The *Vedas* themselves are divided into four texts called *Rig, Sama, Yajur* and *Atharva.* The introductory passages include invocations and hymns dedicated to personified forces of nature and are called *samhitas.* Some portions of the *Vedas* give detailed account of ritual and sacrificial practices and are classed as *karmakanda.* The philosophy or theology of Hinduism is found in the concluding portions of the *Vedas* called the *Upanishads.*

Vanquishing ignorance ~ the *Upanishads*

The word *upanishad* is composed of two Sanskrit roots: *upa* meaning to approach and *shada* implying destruction (of delusion). The inference is that as the individual studies the *Upanishads*, his delusion is destroyed. There are one hundred and eight *Upanishads*, eleven of which are considered to be central. The *Upanishads* expound the essential nature of man as *Atman,* and the essential nature of the cosmos as *Brahman.* The conclusion of Hindu philosophy is that the underpinning to everything is *spiritual.* When the ultimate reality is viewed not as the spirit but as a personality it is addressed as God.

Some *Upanishads* equate *Atman* to *Brahman* since they are both seen as *'essentially the same spirit.'* This implies that God, man and the universe are essentially manifestations of the same Ultimate reality referred to as the spirit. The philosophical elaboration of the *Upanishads* forms the basis of all the *Vedanta* schools of philosophy. Vivekananda said that the *Upanishads* are the "great mine of strength. Therein lies strength enough to invigorate the whole world; the whole world can be vivified, made strong, energised through them."

The synthesis of the *Upanishads* ~ the *Bhagavad Gita*

The *Bhagavad Gita*, literally means 'the song of the divine'; it is the central text of the Hindus. The *Bhagavad Gita* is a spiritual discourse given by *Krishna* at a pivotal point within the great epic, the *Mahabharata*. *Krishna* imparts the essence of *upanishadic* teachings to *Arjuna* on the battlefield and tells him how to translate these lofty teachings into practice. The *Bhagavad Gita* teaches how to use religion in daily context.

The key teaching of the *Bhagavad Gita* can be summed up in one word: 'Renunciation'. We can find God if we stop chasing minor goals. The sacrifice of worldly desires to make spiritual progress paves the way to enlightenment. *Krishna* states: "He whose mind is not attached to anything, who has subdued his heart, and who is free from all longing, he, by renunciation, attains supreme perfection" B.G.18.49. Renunciation can be achieved in many ways (margas). Through selfless action (*karma*), through devotion (bhakti), through psychic control (*raja yoga*), or through the intellect (*jnana*).

In the *Bhagavad Gita, Krishna* expounds the theory of transmigration of souls (reincarnation), the law of *karma,* and the belief that everything is composed of the three attributes (*gunas*). The *Bhagavad Gita* is the summation and synthesis of Hindu beliefs.

The Bhagavad Gita
A spiritual dialogue on the battlefield

Who are we and what is this all about? ~ The six schools of philosophy

There are six schools of philosophy in Hinduism, all endeavouring to offer a rational response to this question. The responses are based on the spiritual experiences of the *rishis*. Three of these schools, *Samkhya, Yoga,* and *Vedanta,* form the basis of modern Hindu philosophy.

Samkhya is believed to be the most ancient philosophic treatise in the world. The author, *Sage Kapila*, endeavoured to determine all the constituents of the universe, incorporating the physical as well as the mental realms. Some of his discoveries are in line with the findings of Quantum Mechanics. *Kapila* taught that we never really experience the objective universe. What we experience is our mind's reaction to the objective universe. Hence the universe we experience is always a fusion of the subject and the object. A unique feature of *Samkhya* is that it is a non-theistic philosophy; meaning that it does not see the need for a 'God' to explain spirituality.

Yoga is the name of another ancient school of philosophy propounded by *Sage Patanjali*. The school of *yoga* philosophy suffuses *Sage Kapila's* findings with the idea of a God in its presentation. The practice of *raja yoga* or meditational discipline as a means to enlightenment is based on the teachings of the *yoga* philosophy. *Raja yoga* can be called an experiment to find God.

Vedanta is considered to be the most contemporary school of Hindu philosophy. The name *Vedanta* translates as the conclusion of the *Vedas*, and consists of the interpretations of *upanishadic* teachings. *Vedanta* is divided into three broad categories:

- **The Synthesis of *Vedanta***
  Dvaita or dualistic *Vedanta* defines God as essentially different from the individual soul. The individual soul strives to love and serve God, thus forming an eternal loving relationship with God. The individual souls, God and Nature are all recognised as everlasting yet distinct from each other. This view is not that different from the Abrahamic approach.

- *Vishisht-Advaita* (qualified non-dualism) teaches that the individual soul and God have a closer link. The individual soul is like a spark and God is like the fire. So they are similar but not quite the same. This stand may be the most practical one. Until one experiences one's identity with God, how can one make such a claim?

- *Advaita* or non-dualistic *Vedanta* promotes the idea that there cannot be more than one ultimate category. If there were more than one such category, they would act to limit each other. *Advaita Vedanta* concludes that the essential nature of God, Man, and the Universe is the same, it is the spirit. The distinctions we experience are confined to the outer manifestations of the spirit. The strength of *Advaita* is that it forms the basis for a link between science and religion.

The Reconciliation of *Vedanta*

The disparities between *Dvaita Vedanta* and *Advaita Vedanta* seem so great that reconciliation may appear impossible. Various religious teachers or *acharyas* have promoted different forms of *Vedanta.* Most Hindus find it easier to conceive of God as a supreme personality to be adored and appeased hence they follow the *dvaita* or *vishisht-advaita* traditions. *Advaita Vedanta* is philosophically more satisfying but it does not offer the support of a Godhead to relate to. It is possible to think of different schools of *Vedanta* as different pathways adopted by different movements to promote spiritual progress. Commenting that one is better than another is going against the grain of the pluralistic teachings of Hinduism.

Ramanuja
Promoted *Vishist-Advaita* ~ you are like God but not quite God.
He is the fire; you are the spark.

Hindu literature ~ the *Smriti* scriptures

The second broad category of Hindu scripture, called the *smritis* is conjectural rather than experiential and therefore bears less authority than the *shruti* scriptures. The word *smriti* means 'that which is remembered', and emphasises that it is man-made literature which was transmitted by memorisation. *Smriti* literature contains many historic and legendary tales presenting religious and philosophic teachings in a narrative format.

The great epics

The two epics, the *Ramayana* and the *Mahabharata,* are considered to be historic stories, though the accuracy of some of the accounts can be questioned as stories have a habit of changing with every telling. The *Ramayana* portrays the life of *Rama* and the *Mahabharata* describes how the *Pandava* brothers overcame adversities with the guidance of *Krishna*. This is one of the longest narrative poems in the world. Both the epics are full of plots and sub-plots, promoting spiritual ideals; offering moral lessons and presenting subtle philosophic ideas in a story format.

The Law books

Also included in the category of *smritis* are law books like the *Manusmriti*. Such books contain codes of conduct for society. *Smriti* literature is only considered relevant within the social contextual framework it was created in. The *Manusmriti* contains rules applicable in India a long time ago, for example sociality based around a hereditary caste system. Such social structures are no longer appropriate or applicable, though they are still in operation in some rural areas in India. *Manu* himself states in his law book that the rules are only applicable within a limited temporal and spatial framework and should be discarded when these bounds are exceeded or if the teachings are in contradiction with the *shrutis*. Because of their relativity, such *smritis* are given inferior status to *shrutis*. The codes of conduct prescribed to modern Hindus come from the heads of contemporary sectarian movements. The best example of this is the *Shiksha Patri,* dictating codes of conduct for the *Swaminarayan* devotees.

The *Mahabharata*
The Epic struggle of the *Pandava* brothers making spiritual progress
while fighting severe adversities

Bringing colour to religion ~ the *Puranas*

Smriti literature contains a vast storehouse of legendary tales presenting ethical and moral teachings in a narrative form. The stories are woven around adventures of various Hindu deities. These stories are referred to as *puranas*. Eighteen of these texts are given prominence and called the *mahapuranas* or great legends. These legends make religions colourful. Although *smriti* literature is subordinate to *shruti* scripture, such *smritis* are seen as essential tools in nurturing love for spirituality and devotion to God. *Smritis* focus on personalities rather than principles, making philosophic ideas appear less abstract. However, if such religious tales are accepted as literal truths, religion immediately comes into conflict with rationality and science.

The *Puranas*
Religion made colourful through narratives

Breadth of vision

No scripture can be 'Absolute'. All scriptures are contextual

Scriptures are essential storehouses of spiritual knowledge for all religions, but none of these scriptures can be classed as 'absolute' else they undermine what they are trying to present. If any religion claims that God has been captured in the scribbles of any text, they destroy the potency of their God. Hindu scriptures pointedly declare: "God is not contained in any of its texts". This is in stark contrast to claims by some theologians of other religions who declare that 'all truths' are captured in their sacred texts.

The Role of Narrative

Philosophy presented in a narrative form is considered to be an essential tool for all religions, thus the role of story telling should never be underestimated. The use of metaphors in religious teachings is not necessarily a weakness but reflects a greater unity operating at a deeper level. Hinduism is not apologetic about its ample use of narrative theology to put across subtle philosophic ideas. Every prophet of every religion has used parables and metaphors to put across their message. All such narratives have to be used judiciously. Modern science uses them too. For example, a scientist will say: "We cannot say that the world is made of quarks but we can explain the world in terms of quarks which are technically a myth - though a very useful myth". The difference between religious myths and scientific myths is that religious myths are set in stone while scientific myths are happy to evolve.

Mythology

Injudicious interpretation of narrative can be very damaging to religions. Mythology presented as literal truth can undermine the validity of religion. Religions are then viewed as irrational and irrelevant by the serious academics. The best example of narrative interpreted as literal truth and thus creating a serious rift between religions and science are the creation stories promoted by many theologians of the Abrahamic religions. The extent to which they are prepared to go to disprove the theory of evolution is a clear case of religions over-stretching their freedom to use narratives.

Memory guide

Shruti	Authoritative Hindu scriptures; the spiritual knowledge acquired through God experience.
Smriti	Narratives to interpret and practise religious teachings
Vedas	Principal *shruti* texts; the books of knowledge
Upanishads	The philosophic portion of the *Vedas*; exploring the essential nature and links between man, God and the universe
Bhagavad Gita	The central scripture of Hindus; teaches how to use religion in daily context and the role of renunciation for spiritual progress
Samkhya School	One of the most ancient philosophies of the world, analysing the world in terms of categories
Yoga School	Uses the teachings of Samkhya and adds category: God
Vedanta School	The most contemporary Hindu school of philosophy; the conclusion of the *Vedas*; based on the *upanishadic* teachings subdivided as follows:
Dvaita Vedanta	Hindu dualism: God as essentially different from the individual and the universe
Vishishtadvaita Vedanta	God is the fire; the individual soul is like a spark
Advaita Vedanta	Non-dualism; sees the essential nature of the individual soul, the universe and God as being non-different
Epics	*Ramayana* and *Mahabharata*
Purana	Legendary stories woven around the adventures of various deities
Law Books	Prescribes codes of conduct for the individual and society

EXTRA NOTES:

Chapter 4
VALUES AND BELIEFS

Reincarnation ~We have lived many lives   (Refer to Chapter 7)
Hindus believe that we are born again and again, this theory is called the theory of reincarnation.

- *Samsara* is the cycle of rebirth and suggests the continuity of our existence beyond death. *Krishna* states in the *Bhagavad Gita* that "as the soul passes in this body through childhood, youth and old age, it also passes through death and takes rebirth in another body." *B.G.*2.13. The only thing that accompanies us into our new life is the character we have built up.

- **There is no Eternal Heaven or Hell** in Hinduism. Just as when we go to sleep and conjure up a dream-world and live in it for a short while, the individual may spend some time between rebirths living in a mental heaven or hell of his own making. There is also reference in the Hindu scriptures that we sometimes share this world with our ancestors, *pitriloka,* or with higher beings *devaloka.* All such interludes are temporary and we continue to be reborn on earth until we attain *moksha.*

- *Moksha:* The cycle of rebirth only comes to an end with *moksha,* liberation from the cycle of rebirth. The word *moksha* derives from two Sanskrit roots: *moha,* meaning delusion and *kshaya* meaning destruction. Hence, *moksha* is the destruction of delusion that takes place when the individual becomes enlightened. *Moksha* is the process of merging with God, or as some would prefer to say 'recognising our identity with God'. The Buddhist word for this is *nirvana,* cessation from rebirth.

- **Evolution:** Hindus believe that at the beginning of the cycle of rebirth we all started off as 'lower beings', originally as a single cell. Over many lifetimes we undergo evolution, as we are reborn into the animal kingdom and then eventually as humans. After the development of human characteristics it would be unlikely (though not impossible) that we may be reborn as an animal or a plant. After being born human, the individual keeps being reborn as human, unless his actions were so bestial as to warrant his being reborn as an animal.

Consequences of the belief in reincarnation:
The positive aspect to the theory of reincarnation is that we can view life as more just. Missed opportunities in one lifetime can perhaps be achieved in another, and rewards not earned in this life may be reaped in another life. The hard work put towards building up character in one life, becomes our asset in the next life.

The drawback with this theory can be that people may adopt a laid-back approach in this life hoping to do better in the following lives. *Moksha,* or liberation, is guaranteed for everyone, so some people may not bother to make spiritual progress in this life. Such a 'laissez-faire' attitude can slow down our spiritual progress.

Reincarnation
We continue to go round the cycle of birth and death until we become mature and search for a way out

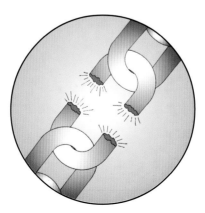

Moksha **(freedom)**
Mature man seeks freedom rather than pleasure

Universal components ~ the three Gunas

Hindus believe that the whole cosmos, including all living and non-living things, is composed of three attributes called the *gunas*. The word *guna* translates as 'thread'. The implication is that the intertwining of these three threads forms the basis of everything. The attributes of these *gunas* are evident in the physical universe as well as in the mental and spiritual realms.

- *Tamas* the first *guna,* which in physical terms is seen as the quality of inertia and darkness. Matter exhibits the inertial quality of *tamas. Tamas* in human terms manifests as laziness and dullness and in the spiritual realm it manifests as ignorance and wrong beliefs.
- *Rajas* the second *guna* is evident in physical terms as forces causing motion. In human terms, *rajas* becomes action, and in the spiritual realm it manifests as passion.
- *Sattva* the third quality and appears in physical terms as the quality of balance and light. *Sattva* in human terms manifests as contentment. In the spiritual realm *sattva* manifests as illumination and knowledge. Spiritual individuals are recognised as being predominantly *sattvic*.

How to use this classification for spiritual progress?

The *Bhagavad Gita* emphasises that first we have to shift from being *tamasic* to being *rajasic,* and finally to become predominantly *sattvic* by developing attributes like contentment thus moving towards spiritual illumination.

The Law of Karma ~ What we sow is what we reap

The Law of *Karma* is also called the law of action and its consequences. Hindus believe that the law of cause and effect is imbedded in the structure of the universe and effects all of us even at an individual level. We have to bear the consequences of our activities or *karma*. In some cases the consequences become evident immediately, in some cases it may take some time for the results of our action to come to fruition. For example, heavy smoking may not produce immediate results but may cause serious illness in a few years time. Hindus take this idea further and say that every action we do will produce consequences, and some will only become evident in our next life or lives. This theory is called the 'law of *karma*.' We reap what we sow and must therefore act with great care. Poor behaviour will produce harmful consequences and disciplined behaviour will produce beneficial results. Recognising a link between our actions and its consequences is a very logical way of promoting better behaviour.

Consequences of belief in the Law of Karma:

- **We are put in charge of our destiny:** The endearing aspect of this theory is that it puts every individual in charge of his own destiny and makes him behave in a focused manner.
- **No God sitting in judgement:** This concept also eliminates the idea of God sitting in judgement. Hindus cannot accept the idea of God sitting in judgement and dishing out punishment at the end of our lives. At worst, we can blame Him for creating the law of cause and effect but then we are put in charge of our destiny and made responsible for what we do. We have to be ready to bear the full consequences of all our actions.

- **The Problem of Indifference:** The law of *karma, if misunderstood*, can have detrimental effects on people's behaviour. For example it can make one indifferent to the suffering of others. Misinterpreting the law of *karma* can result in people not helping others in distress, who supposedly 'deserve to suffer' due to their past wrong actions. This indifferent attitude to others' suffering can inadvertently have negative effect on one's own *karma*. The correct interpretation of the law of *karma* would require one not to ignore the suffering of others, but help to alleviate it, thus acquiring good *karma* for oneself in the process.

- **Fatalism:** The law of *karma* can also be misinterpreted in another way. Some individuals may become indifferent to their *own* suffering. They may not attempt to recover from their unfortunate circumstances but wallow in them since they 'deserve to suffer' for their former misdeeds. This apathy towards improving one's condition is called *fatalism*. The correct interpretation of the law of *karma* does not advocate any such idea. To the contrary, it would suggest that rather than blame one's past *karma*, one should fight back and negate the results of earlier bad *karma* by performing good *karma*.

Karma
disciplined actions produce beneficial results

Everything is sacred ~ *Ahimsa*

Ahimsa is the Sanskrit word for 'non-violence' and forms the central doctrine of Hindu teachings on morality. This concept arises most naturally from *Advaita,* or the non-dualistic philosophy of Hinduism. This philosophy teaches that the universe and all living things are expressions of the spirit, *Brahman*. It further teaches that living beings, especially mankind, is the clearest manifestation of the spirit. When we hurt someone we are essentially hurting ourselves, since at a deeper level we are essentially the same. Thus all living things are respected. The inanimate universe is also revered as sacred; it too is the expression of the divine.

Some things are more sacred than others

This theory promotes a hierarchy: living beings are more sacred than non-living things, as the spirit is more clearly visible in them. Among living beings, a further hierarchy is put into place. Human life is seen as more valuable than animal or plant life, as divinity has become more manifest in human life through the process of evolution. The whole universe is called *shrishti* or a projection of God. All animate as well as inanimate objects must be treated with reverence, as everything is a manifestation of God. This places an added responsibility on mankind. Human beings are at the top of the evolutionary scale and are seen as the stewards of creation. They are responsible for protecting all life forms and the environment. The practice of *ahimsa* emanates unequivocally from *Advaita,* as seen in the *upanishadic* phrase: *Isha vasyam idam sarvam* "perceive all this as God." *Ish Up. 1.*

Ahimsa in the *Dvaita* tradition

Ahimsa in the *Dvaita* philosophy is presented in a slightly different way. The *Dvaita* tradition, like the *Abrahamic* traditions, sees man and God as separate. It teaches that, as God created all living things, they should be treated with compassion and not harmed otherwise God will be displeased. This idea is put into practise through *daya,* compassion, and *dana,* charity. In this instance *Ahimsa* does not arise naturally but it has to be *imposed* on mankind as a commandment from God.

Ahimsa
The positive interpretation of *Ahimsa* is
'Reverence for all living beings'

The Influence of *Ahimsa* on dietary practices

Hindus do not insist on vegetarianism but recommend it very highly. Vegetarianism practised by Hindus is likely to be a legacy from the Buddhist and Jain traditions that laid great emphasis on the principle of *ahimsa*. For example, *Buddha* stated that "Goodwill towards all beings is the true religion; cherish in your hearts boundless goodwill to all that lives." *Buddha* is recognised as the personification of compassion and Hindus revere him as an *avatar*. He was prepared to lay down his life to save an animal.

Mahavira
Reverence not reserved for a God in the heavens but
shown towards all living beings

The Jain religion does not express spirituality through the idea of a deity (a God) but through reverence for all living beings. Reverence for an imagined being residing in some distant plane is transferred to reverence for all living things here and now. **Jain** teachings give the principal of *ahimsa* as much prominence as the concept of God in other religions; the practice and principle of *ahimsa* are taken to its apex by this religion. The Jain founders were called *jinas,* the victorious ones, the most famous *jina* being *Mahavira* (599-527BC). Jain practices of *ahimsa* include abstention from eating after nightfall to avoid accidental consumption of any insects, and abstention from pulling out and eating root vegetables, as this may involve killing organisms living underground.

Some Hindus are meat eaters

Some Hindus have always consumed meat and continue to do so. Though the hierarchy for reverence to life in the Hindu tradition strongly suggests that if we are able to live on plant life, we should avoid eating meat. The cruelty suffered by animals reared for human consumption should be reason enough for anyone not to consume meat. Recent medical findings also clearly show the greater benefits of a vegetarian diet.

Man's best friend is the humble cow

Hindus would disagree with the English who claim that man's best friend is the dog. Since the dawn of civilisation one animal stands out as a special friend of man. This animal is the humble cow. No other animal has been such a loyal and gentle provider to mankind. When we want to extend the idea of reverence for life into the animal kingdom, the most appropriate candidate to receive our reverence has to be the cow. Hence Hindus do not eat beef. There is another reason why the cow holds a special place in Hinduism. *Krishna* as a cowherd boy had shown great tenderness towards the cows he looked after. Hindus therefore revere this animal and give it a sacred status.

The Humble Cow
This gentle provider is man's best friend

The Cruel treatment of animals bred for human consumption

The amount of suffering endured by animals bred for human consumption or the poor condition in which they are kept, transported and slaughtered is well documented. Many people in the West are becoming vegetarian as they are appalled at the level of cruelty suffered by so many animals.

Should we experiment on live animals? (Vivisection)

Cruelty suffered by animals used for experimentation is also a serious issue that needs to be addressed. Though human life is considered to be more valuable than animal life, can this justify carrying out experiments on live animals for medical breakthroughs? Hinduism cannot offer a clear directive. If the experiments are conducted just to assist the cosmetic industry then the answer would certainly be no; but if such research can produce cures for serious diseases suffered by mankind, then it becomes difficult to offer a clear directive.

The Idea of *Ahimsa* extended to care for the environment

The positive aspect highlighted by the concept of *ahimsa* is *reverence for everything*. This includes the environment. Mankind is becoming very aware of the need to care for the environment. Due to our greed and carelessness we may do irrevocable damage to our planet. The consequences will be felt by future generations. Society is becoming aware of these issues and is making efforts in the following areas:

- Using lesser amounts of fossil fuels
- Using energy saving devices
- Looking for alternate sources of energy
- Raising public awareness
- Recycling raw material more vigorously

The Spiritual reason for conserving the environment

The reason why we should look after the environment is not only a matter of practical concern but a matter of spiritual concern as taught by the first verse of the *Isha Upanishad* 'View and treat everything as divine'. Hindus say that the reason why we should not poison our planet is because the planet is *essentially* God.

Gandhi politicises *Ahimsa*

Gandhi, the famous political activist of the last century was greatly influenced by the Hindu and Jain teachings of truth, *satya,* and non-violence, *ahimsa*. He utilised these two spiritual ideals in politics, and coined a phrase *satyagraha*, which meant 'insistence on truth' in a non-violent manner. *Gandhi* also insisted on *swaraj* or self-rule for Indians in order to overthrow the British rule in India. The methods he employed emphasised the role of non-violence: *ahimsa paramo dharma*, "non-violence is the highest religion". His ideas were successfully utilised to secure independence for India in a non-violent manner. This is a unique achievement in the history of mankind as a major political change took place with little or no violence. Though some would argue that the violence that erupted between Hindus and Muslims after the Indian independence marred this achievement.

Ahimsa in context

However, it should not be forgotten that *ahimsa* can only be practised in certain circumstances. If for example, Hitler were ruling India, *Gandhi* would not have been successful. Hinduism recognises that in many circumstances, it may be necessary to make a show of force, and in some cases even resort to force to resolve serious issues. Religions have to be practised in context. There cannot be any 'absolute' dictate applicable to everyone in all circumstances, even when it comes to translating the ideal of *ahimsa* into practise. This is clearly evident in the teachings of the *Bhagavad Gita* where *Krishna* encourages *Arjuna* to fight and destroy the wrongdoers. Religion practised in context is called **Varnashrama dharma.** A Hindu monk would be advised not to react in a violent manner under any circumstances, while a householder would be advised to fight to defend his family.

Gandhi
Managed to use spiritual tools for political ends

Ahimsa on an international scale

Gandhi's success in adopting the method of 'non-violent resistance' to gain independence for India is a unique phenomenon in the history of mankind.

Gandhi believed that "non-violence is infinitely superior to violence, forgiveness is more manly than punishment, forgiveness adorns the soldier". Individuals or groups fighting for a common cause, or whole nations seeking political resolution, can now try out this idea of fighting injustice in a non-violent manner. In the nineteen sixties, *Martin Luther King,* the black activist leader in the United States, put *Gandhi's* principles into practice and gained equal rights for the black people. *Martin Luther King* stated that "to be a follower of the principle of *ahimsa* one has to be a true hero". *Desmond Tutu* in South Africa also adopted *Gandhi's* principle of non-violent resistance. In the long term this method succeeded in replacing the *apartheid* system of government with a democratic one. Many individuals and groups fighting for justice have successfully used non-violent protest to secure justice.

Breadth of vision

The three *Gunas* in Physics
Newton's laws of motion can be seen as the codification of the three *gunas* in Physics. The first law defines the concept of inertia in matter, *tamas.* The second law defines force as bringing about a change in the state of an object, *rajas.* The third law expresses the idea of balance: equality between action and reaction, *sattva.*

Reincarnation
The theory of reincarnation gives a better explanation to phenomena such as phobias or geniuses. It also provides a more just worldview, offering chances for everyone to better themselves. However it can also result in a 'laid-back' attitude to spiritual progress.

The Law of *Karma*
Unfortunately, most textbooks on Hinduism have seriously misinterpreted this law. They state that the cause of 'suffering' is the law of *karma.* Causality can be foolishly blamed for every phenomenon under the sun including suffering, as it is the essential link between all objects and events. The second volume in this series tackles this issue in detail.

Ahimsa
Ahimsa can only be practised in context. Some people can take the practice of *ahimsa* to the extreme by not taking antibiotic remedies to fight off infection. The question still remains as to what extent can one truly practise *ahimsa.* The very process of breathing destroys millions of organisms in our lungs, so should we stop breathing? It should be left to the individual to decide to what extent he wants to practise *ahimsa.*

A show of violence, as opposed to being violent, is a useful stance to adopt. This principle is called *hiss but do not bite*. It can be used to resolve many difficult situations without resorting to violence.

Sometimes cowardice can parade as *ahimsa.* There is a big difference between the practitioners of *ahimsa* such as *Gandhi* or *Martin Luther King,* who gave their lives for their beliefs, and others, who may be looking for an excuse to hide their cowardice.

Memory guide

Gunas	Universal constituents; three threads that weave the fabric of the universe
Tamas	Inertia, darkness, laziness, dullness, ignorance
Rajas	Force, motion, activity, passion
Sattva	Balance, light, contentment, peace, illumination
Samsara	The cycle of rebirth; suggesting continuity of our existence after death
Nirvana	A Buddhist term; cessation of the cycle of rebirth
Law of Karma	The law of cause and effect on personal terms; we have to bear the consequences of all our actions
Ahimsa	Non-killing; non-violence; reverence for everything
Shrishti	A projection; universe is a projection of *Brahman*
Buddha	The enlightened one; founder of Buddhism; personification of compassion; 9th *avatar* of *Vishnu*
Mahavira	Key founder of Jainism: personification of *ahimsa*
Gandhi	Political activist, used spiritual ideas of *satya*, truth and *ahimsa* non-violence to gain independence for India
Satyagraha	'Insistence on truth'; a tool used by *Gandhi* as a means of non-violent struggle against the British rule in India
Swaraj	'Self rule'
Martin Luther King	Black civil rights leader who adopted *Gandhi's* methods to gain equal rights for the black people in the USA
Desmond Tutu	A South African Christian leader who also adopted *Gandhi's* methods of non-violent resistance

EXTRA NOTES:

Chapter 5
RELIGION IN DAILY LIFE

Why bother with rituals at all?

Rituals are essentially a means of reminding ourselves of the spiritual dimension we possess. If we do not follow some kind of ritual, we may end up by losing sight of higher goals in life.

- Some rituals, such as prayer or worship, remind us of God on a daily basis.
- Other rituals, such as fasting or meditation, are a way of disciplining our lives for spiritual progress.
- Some rituals, for example the celebration of festivals, the observance of religious ceremonies, or pilgrimage, become important events that help us focus our minds on religious aspirations.

Remembering God through worship ~ *puja* in the home

Hindus define any activity that draws them to God, as 'worship'. The traditional worship ceremony is called a *puja* from the Sanskrit root *pu* implying 'adoration' or 'worship'. Though there are no hard and fast rules about how to do worship, there are some guidelines. Dawn and dusk are recommended as the most suitable times for daily *puja,* as at this time, everything is naturally very calm and peaceful.

A shrine may be placed in an allocated room or an area of the home set aside for the *puja* ceremony. An image or *murti* of the presiding family deity is placed on a well-decorated and elevated platform. Normally one of the family members carries out the worship ceremony using several artefacts.

Rituals
Expression of spirituality in daily life

Puja:

- First, water is sprinkled around the shrine area as a symbol of purification.
- A lamp or *diva* is lit to represent transition from darkness or ignorance to light.
- A *tilak* is a mark made on the forehead between the eyebrows to signify the individual's aspiration for spiritual awakening.
- Flowers may be offered to symbolise the devotees' offering of their heart to God.
- Fruit or food may be offered to the deity as a sign of gratitude.
- Incense, which is also lit, releases a scent that permeates the room, symbolising that God permeates the universe.
- A bell is rung to draw the mind away from sounds that may distract from the *puja.* The sweet tinkling sound of the bell keeps the worshippers' mind focused on the *puja.*
- Camphor, a white paraffin-like substance is burnt to symbolise the destruction of the ego.

The Arti or welcoming ceremony, is the focal activity in the *puja*. A lamp is placed on a tray and waved in a clockwise direction in front of the image. During this process, the worshippers may sing invocational hymns as a way of welcoming God. Other activities during the *puja* ceremony may include meditation, singing, chanting, scriptural reading and telling beads. When the *puja* ceremony is over, the devotee bows down to the image. The fruit and food that has been offered to the deity is now called *prashad,* sanctified food to be distributed and consumed by everyone.

Communal worship in the temple

Hindus consider the temple or the *mandir* as the earthly home of God. There are thousands of temples in India and other parts of the world, each dedicated to a particular Hindu deity. The *mandir* characteristically has a *shikhar*, similar to a steeple, symbolising high mountains where spirituality was practised in the past. The inner shrine where the central deities are housed is called the *garba-griha*. Adjoining most temples is a *natamandir,* a community meeting place used for various religious activities.

Many devotees flock to these temples to obtain *darshan* or vision of their chosen deity.

Visiting the Temple:

- Traditionally, devotees only enter the temple after taking ablutions and may bring with them some form of offering, usually flowers or fruit.
- Shoes are removed at the entrance of the temple to prevent dirt getting into the inner areas of the temple.
- The devotee then rings a bell situated at the front of the temple to announce his presence to God.
- The devotee bows down to the image to pay obeisance and presents his offerings.
- The role of the temple priest (often a *brahmin*) is to carry out the *puja* ritual. The *arti* ceremony in the temple is a more elaborate ceremony and may involve lighting five lamps arranged on a tray to symbolise worship through the five elements.
- The congregation in the temple will often sing devotional compositions called *bhajans,* accompanied by musical instruments like cymbals, drums, and harmonium.
- At the end of the *puja* ceremony, the *arti* tray is passed round the congregation. Each person cups his hands over the flames and then passes his hands over his heart and head as a way of accepting God's blessings.
- The devotee may also circumambulate or walk around the deity in a clockwise direction so as to keep God on his 'right side.' At the end of the worship ceremony, the food offered to the deity is distributed as *prashad.*

Flexibility in all ceremonials:

Hinduism allows a great deal of flexibility in the way all rituals are performed, since it is not the elaborate or meticulous ceremony that counts, but the heartfelt love of the devotee that is important. As *Krishna* teaches in the *Bhagavad Gita*: "Whatever is offered to me with love; a fruit or a flower or a leaf, I readily accept." 9.26 It is a pity that some Hindus take advantage of this flexibility and end up by abandoning rituals all together. Rituals are a very important way of reminding ourselves of our spiritual aspirations.

The mark of a Hindu ~ the *Tilak*

Hindus often use a *tilak*, a mark made on the forehead, to reflect their religious allegiance. The *Yoga* school believes that when a person becomes enlightened he experiences a spiritual sensation between his eyebrows. Hence this spot is marked externally as a symbol for awakening spirituality.

The sectarian allegiance expressed by the *Tilak*

The *tilak* also gives a sense of belonging and kinship to the devotee; in some cases the particular form of the *tilak* may reflect his allegiance to a particular sectarian movement within Hinduism.

- The worshippers of *Vishnu,* called *Vaishnavites,* apply a U shape *tilak* made with sandal paste on their foreheads; the shape represents the 'footprint' of *Vishnu.*
- The devotees of *Shiva,* called *Shaivites* use sacred ash called *bhasma,* to mark their foreheads. The three horizontal lines they mark across the forehead represent mastery over the physical, mental and spiritual realms.
- Devotees of the Mother Goddess, *shaktas,* apply a round red dot on their foreheads. The colour red is associated with feminine power, *Shakti.*

Tilak
The mark of a Hindu, spiritual as well as ornamental

Celebrating Festivals

Celebrating festivals is a joyous way in which religious communities remind themselves of their spiritual aspirations.

Festivals in all religions can be classed into three broad categories:

- Festivals that celebrate historic or mythological events like the birth of an important religious personality.
- Festivals that celebrate personal relationships.
- Festivals that celebrate seasonal changes.

Religious festivals are joyous occasions when good food is prepared and eaten (though some devotees may decide to fast as an austerity practised on the day). Everyone wears their best clothes and enjoys the opportunity of meeting other members of their family or community. During some festivities, presents may be exchanged, and people may attend special events commemorating the event.

The birth of *Krishna* ~ *Janmasthami*

Hindus celebrate the birth of *Krishna* at *Janmasthami,* which means 'birth on the eighth day'. *Krishna* was born on the eighth day of the Indian month of *Shravan* at midnight. Many devotees fast all day and celebrate the birth at midnight. Children may enact stories of *Krishna* and adults may sing the glories of *Krishna* on this day. *Krishna* is the most famous deity of the Hindus and is worshipped on this day in the form of a *baby.*

The birth of *Rama* ~ *Ramanavami*

Rama's birth is celebrated on *Ramanavami.* The day falls on the ninth day of the month of *Chaitra.* During the eight days prior to the birth, many devotees fast, and spend time listening to the recitals of the epic *Ramayana.* *Rama* was born at mid-day so the main celebrations and worship take place in homes and temples at midday. The celebrations may involve children enacting stories from the *Ramayana* and devotees may recite and sing the glories of *Rama.*

Baby *Krishna*
God worshipped as a child

The bond of protection ~ *Raksha-bandhan*

Certain Hindu festivals honour human relationships, such as *Raksha-bandhan.* The word *raksha-bandhan* means 'a thread for protection'. On this auspicious day, a sister ties a thread around her brother's right wrist to highlight the special relationship between a brother and a sister. The brother in turn offers a gift to his sister. The thread stands for protection from adversities but more importantly it stands for 'special human relationships.' Any female can tie this thread around the wrist of any male, raising their relationship to a platonic level.

Guru purnima
Celebrates the bond between a teacher and his students

Reverence for teachers ~ *Guru-purnima*

The relationship between a *guru,* the spiritual teacher and the student, is considered to be very sacred. The *guru* is respected as the human intermediary between man and God. On this day, the student will visit and pay obeisance to his teacher; he may offer some gifts and ask for his blessings. Respecting the teacher may appear old-fashioned but is relevant in our times. It in an indirect way of paying tribute to the process of transmitting knowledge.

Bring colour to life ~ *Holi*

Holi is a Hindu festival celebrating the arrival of spring. This festival also commemorates a mythological event relating to *Prahlad*, a child devotee of *Vishnu*. On this day, *Vishnu* saved *Prahlad* from being burnt alive by *Holika*, a demoness, hence *Holi* is the name given to this festival.

Traditionally a bonfire is lit and foodstuff such as grains, coconuts and dates are offered to it. The coconut is sometimes roasted and later distributed as sanctified food, *prashad*. Newly born babies are especially taken to witness the event in order to receive *Vishnu's* blessings and protection. On the following day called *Dhuleti*, people celebrate the arrival of spring by showering coloured water and powder on each other. The arrival of spring means the arrival of colour to the landscape and is seen as a time for rejoicing.

Holi
Marks the arrival of spring; celebrated with a bonfire

A row of lights to welcome *Rama* ~ *Diwali*

Diwali, the festival of lights, is the most famous festival in the Hindu calendar and takes place at the beginning of winter. It commemorates the night *Rama* returned home after fourteen years in exile. On this historic night, there was no moonlight, hence the citizens of his hometown *Ayodhya*, lit up the streets with many oil lamps or *divas* to welcome Him home. The *diva* has become the emblem of the festival. The word *Dipawali* is the correct name for *Diwali* meaning 'a row of lights'.

At *Diwali*, Hindus also celebrate *Lakshmi Puja*, the worship of the goddess of prosperity. *Puja* is carried out in the home with all the family members and may be led by a priest. This is accompanied by the exchange of gifts, new clothes, sweets and money, and culminates in a lavish feast. Charitable activities are also performed on this auspicious day. Business people worship their books on this day as a way of showing respect to their trade in a ceremony called *Chopra Pujan.* At night, there may be firework displays. The day after *Diwali* is the Hindu New Year; on this day resolutions are made and greetings exchanged.

Diwali
Festival celebrated with fireworks

Victory of good over evil ~ *Navaratri* and *Durga-puja*

The word *Navaratri* means 'nine nights' and is the name of the festival that marks the advent of autumn. The event also marks the nine days *Rama* fought the demon *Ravana* with the blessings of the Mother Goddess *Durga*. *Rama* defeated the demon *Ravana* on the tenth day of *Dusshera*, sometimes called the 'day of victory' *Vijaya Dashami*.

According to another narrative, it is also the time when the Mother Goddess *Durga* fought a demon called *Mahisasura* for nine days. Symbolically the event celebrates the victory of good over evil by invoking strength, *shakti*.

Every night, for the nine nights of *Navaratri*, devotees gather together for folk dances called *garba,* which take place in a circle around the image of the Mother Goddess. Nearly all Hindus, young and old, male and female, participate in this annual event. Fruit and food is offered to the Mother Goddess and distributed to everybody at the end as *Prashad*. Since these are auspicious days in the Hindu calendar, it is traditional for many women to fast during this period. *Dusshera*, the tenth day, is the day when special worship of the Mother Goddess takes place, called *Durga Puja*. To commemorate the victory of good over evil, an effigy of the demon *Ravana* is set alight.

Garba
Communal dance as a way of showing devotion to the Mother Goddess

**Pilgrimage ~ A Spiritual journey;
but why go on a pilgrimage?** Pilgrimage is a spiritual journey called *yatra*. Like other rituals, *yatra* reminds the devotee of God, and acts as a discipline for spiritual progress. Going on pilgrimage can be a lifelong wish for many Hindus, and may be undertaken as an austerity that culminates in gaining *darshan*, or vision of their chosen deity. Going on pilgrimage is not compulsory for Hindus but can be carried out to obtain merit or good *karma* for oneself.

Pilgrimage
A spiritual journey

Places of pilgrimage are called *tirtha*, which literally means a 'crossing-over point'. The implication is that places of pilgrimage is where the individual can cross over from the physical world into the spiritual world.

Choice of places for pilgrimage:

- Some locations are chosen as suitable sites for pilgrimage because they are geographically significant; for example, vast mountain ranges such as the *Himalayas,* or rivers like the *Ganges*. These places can make the devotee feel spiritually uplifted by gazing at their grandeur.
- Other places become sites for pilgrimage because they are historically important. A saint or a Godly person may have been born or may have lived at a particular location, which then becomes sacred, for example *Ayodhya* where *Rama* ruled, or *Vrindavan* where *Krishna* grew up as a child.
- Sites may also be chosen if they are referred to in mythological stories, for example, *Mysore* is referred to as the place where the demon *Mahisasura* was slain by the Mother Goddess.

Himalayas
Highest peaks inspiring the highest ideals

What to do there?
The purpose of going on a pilgrimage is to spur the devotee into making spiritual progress. At places of pilgrimage, the devotee may spend time in quiet contemplation, in carrying out charitable tasks, or by spending time in the company of holy men. However, there is always the risk that the process degenerates and turns into a sight seeing expedition. It can be argued that money spent on such lavish and expensive trips could be better spent on charitable work.

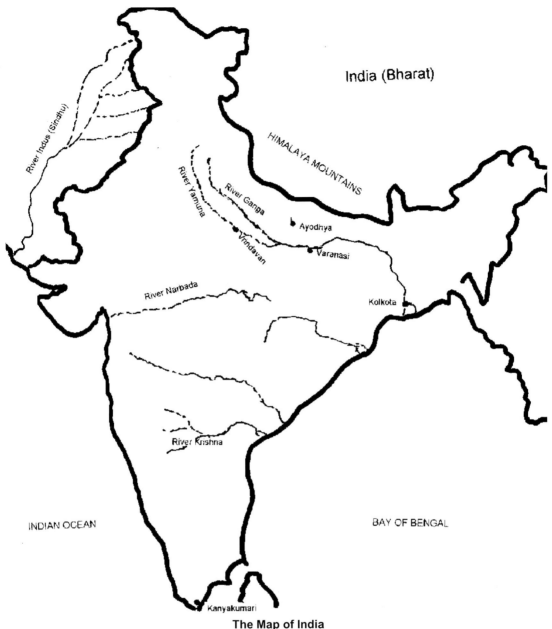

India (Bharat)

The Map of India
The Main rivers and some of the places of pilgrimage

The abode of *Shiva ~ Varanasi*

Varanasi is the most popular pilgrimage site in India. It has geographic, historic as well as mythological significance. *Varanasi* is the place where two tributaries of the river *Ganges*, called *Varaha* and *Asi* meet. The town is situated on the banks of the river *Ganges*, and Hindu narrative suggests that it is the abode of *Shiva* on earth. There are multiple *Shiva* temples in *Varanasi*, the principal being the *Vishvanath Temple*. Pilgrims can visit these temples to obtain *darshan* of *Shiva* as well as take ablutions in the river *Ganges* to symbolically wash away their sins. Many Hindus believe that if a person dies in *Varanasi*, they immediately attain *moksha* or liberation from the cycle of rebirth. This is perhaps one of the reasons why the ashes of the deceased are brought here and immersed in the river. *Varanasi* is historically significant as it is considered to be one of the most ancient seats of learning in India. Almost all ancient and modern proponents of Hinduism have either visited or given spiritual discourses at *Varanasi*, hence the atmosphere is said to be charged with their dynamism.

The River *Ganges* is the most sacred river in Hinduism. It flows from the *Himalayas* right across the northern part of India till it reaches the Bay of Bengal. A dip in the river symbolically washes away the sins of the devotee. There is a story about *Ganga*, a Goddess who can purify, descending to earth to wash away the sins of mankind. Can a dip in a holy river actually wash away our sins? Sri Ramakrishna explains in a humorous manner, "When the devotee takes a dip, his sins just perch on the branches of the tree nearby and jump back on his shoulder when he comes out."

Varanasi
The Abode of *Shiva* on the banks of the holy river *Ganges*

Sri Rama's city ~ *Ayodhya*

Ayodhya is situated along the banks of the river *Saryu* in *Uttar Pradesh* in Northern India. It is a sanctified place since it is the birthplace of *Rama* and also the capital of the kingdom he ruled over. Pilgrims and inhabitants can visit the multiple temples and sites associated with the life of *Rama* as well as circumambulate (go around) the city, as a way of acquiring merit and paying respect to this *avatar*. Many holy men reside in *Ayodhya* and can be visited for spiritual guidance and blessings. Some pilgrims decide to perform charitable deeds in this holy city, such as feeding and clothing the needy.

Dip in the holy river *Ganges*
Can this really wash away our sins?

Unfortunately, *Ayodhya* has recently become a place of political turmoil, due to a controversy surrounding a mosque called the *Babri Masjid*. A Muslim emperor called *Babar* deliberately built the mosque right on top of the site marking the birthplace of *Rama*. Many Hindus wanting to rebuild a temple at this location have demolished the mosque, creating tension between Hindus and Muslims.

Sri Krishna's divine sport at *Vrindavan*

Vrindavan is located on the banks of one of the main rivers in Northwest India called the *Jamuna*, which later along its course joins up with the river *Ganges*. *Vrindavan* is also in the vicinity of a larger town called *Mathura*, where *Krishna* was born. *Krishna* grew up in a small village nearby called *Gokul*, and sported as a young boy in *Vrindavan*. There are many sacred sites in *Vrindavan* linked to the stories of *Krishna*. For example the *Kaliaghat* is a place along the banks of the river where *Krishna* overpowered a giant serpent called *Kalia*. It is also believed that *Krishna* lifted the *Govardhan* mountain with his finger to protect the villagers from heavy rains.

Many temples dedicated to *Krishna* have been built in and around *Vrindavan,* like the famous *Banke-Bihari* temple. Devotees would visit these temples for gaining *darshan* (sight) of *Krishna*. They may visit some of the locations linked with the childhood adventures of *Krishna*. Many devotees of *Krishna* choose to spend their final days in *Vrindavan* hoping to be liberated from the cycle of re-birth by dying in this sanctified place. Pilgrims can meet many holy men and women who live in *Vrindaavan* and visit some of the many *ashramas* or hermitages established here.

Krishna
Lifts the Govardhan mountain to protect the villagers

Samskara
Rituals to mark entry into different stages of life

Rites of Passage ~ *Samskaras*

The word *samskara* should not be confused with the word *samsara*. *Samskara* means 'mental impressions' and means 'rites or rituals performed to instil good impressions'. *Samskaras* are rites of passage or 'sacraments'. Hindu scriptures mention sixteen *samskaras*, which are religious ceremonies marking entry into different stages of life. The initial *samskara* is performed for the individual even before he is conceived, and the final rite takes place after he has passed away. In modern times, the individual may only perform a few of the 16 *samskaras*. All rituals are important if they are performed with proper understanding, but there is always a danger that they could degenerate and become purely mechanical activities, thus losing their significance.

A child is named ~ *Namakarana*

Namakarana means naming ceremony and is one of the earliest *samskaras* performed when the child is around eleven days old. The paternal aunt customarily has the privilege of naming the child, however the first letter of the name is determined by an astrological chart drawn up for the baby. The chosen name is whispered into the child's ear or written in honey on the child's tongue. Names are traditionally chosen to reflect spiritual aspirations, such as *Kripa*, meaning 'grace'. Sometimes names express natural beauty for example *Pushpa*, meaning 'flower'. It is also customary to choose one of the names of Hindu Gods or Goddesses like *Rama* or *Shiva* or *Durga* for the child. This would mean that every time the child is addressed, family members inadvertently repeat the name of God.

Namakarana
Naming the child

The child enters the student stage ~ *Upanayana*

The word *upanayana* literally means 'approaching God' and is a ceremony marking entry into the student stage of life. The ceremony is performed when the child is about eight years old. This ceremony is also referred to as the 'sacred thread ceremony', as the youngster is invested with a sacred thread, consisting of three strands. This is placed on the left shoulder and goes diagonally across the body. The three strands stand for the youngster's duties to his parents, teachers and God. A sacred fire or *havan* is lit and the father or priest whispers the *gayatri*, the main prayer of the Hindu tradition, into the child's ear to mark his entry into religious life. He is now considered to be ready to study the scriptures and carry out the worship ceremony at the family shrine. The youngster is expected to lead a celibate lifestyle, called *brahmacharya*, till he completes his education. In ancient times, girls were also invested with the sacred thread; there is no reason why they should not be encouraged to participate in this ceremony in modern times.

Upanayana
The sacred thread ceremony

Ready to bear the burden of the household ~ *Vivah*

The word *vivah* implies 'bearing a burden'. *Vivah* is the marriage ceremony that marks the individual's transition from the student stage to the householder's stage of life.

Details of the wedding ceremony:

- *Panigrahana:* The ritual includes *panigrahana*: the bride's father offering the hand of the bride to the groom.
- **Exchanging vows with fire as the witness:** A *havan* or fire is lit and the priest recites the relevant hymns from the scriptures. The bride and groom offer *ghee:* clarified butter, and grains to the fire to seek the blessings of 'higher beings.' The fire deity, *Agni,* is regarded as the witness to the wedding ceremony. The bride and groom walk together around the sacred fire four times; after every turn, the bride places her right foot on a piece of rock to symbolise her steadfastness in fulfilling her role as a wife.
- *Saptapadi:* At the end of the ceremony the couple take seven steps together; each step represents strivings for their married life. The first step is taken for God; the

Vivah
Marriage vows of lifelong friendship

others are for health, wealth, strength, children and happiness. The final step represents lifelong friendship between the husband and wife.
- **Marking the forehead:** The bride's forehead is then marked with red powder called *kumkum*. As a blessing, the couple is showered with rice and petals, the wife is now referred to as the *sahadharmini,* the 'companion for spiritual progress.' The ceremony emphasises spiritual as well as material goals.

The final rites ~ *Antima Kriya*

This is the sixteenth and final *samskara* and involves the cremation of the body. Cremation is performed rather than burial in the Hindu tradition. The *Bhagavad Gita* refers to the body as an outer garment of the individual soul; when this garment becomes old or diseased it has to be discarded for a new one. It is not believed that the body 'contains' any aspect of the individual after his death. Hence the body is not preserved but cremated.

Firstly, the body is bathed and clothed. For Hindus living in the West, the body is then placed in a coffin and taken to the crematorium. Verses from the *Bhagavad Gita,* about the immortality of the soul are chanted at the time of cremation to comfort the mourning relatives. The verses expound that the essential nature of man is the *Atman,* which does not die with the body. After the cremation, the remains are collected and placed in an urn. They may then be taken for immersion in the sea or river, or scattered in some holy place. The family usually mourns for a period of thirteen days. At the end of this period the family will conduct a *shradh* ceremony involving giving alms and feeding holy men.

Four Ashramas	Brahmacharya	Grihastha
	Vanaprastha	Sanyasa

Putting ideals into practice ~ the four *Ashramas*

The word *ashrama* is derived from the Sanskrit root *shrama* meaning 'that which has to be achieved through effort'. *Ashrama* can also mean a 'hermitage', but here it signifies the Hindu division of life into four stages. This system enables the individual to fulfil the four aims of human life.

Four aims of life: These are righteous living, *dharma*, the aquisition of wealth, *artha*, the satiation of legitimate desires, *kama,* and finally liberation from the cycle of rebirth, *moksha*. By putting in the necessary effort, *shrama,* a Hindu hopes to achieve these four aims of life.

Four stages of life: The four *ashramas* are called the student stage, *brahmacharya,* the householder stage, *grihastha,* the forest-dweller's stage, *vanaprastha* and the stage of renunciation, *sanyasa*. Since medieval times, the Hindus have abandoned this practice but the values promoted in each of the four stages are still very relevant and should be incorporated into modern living.

Brahmacharya
A celibate lifestyle of self-discipline and dignity

The first stage of life focuses on celibacy, study and respect ~ *brahmacharya*

The word *brahmacharya* is composed of two Sanskrit words: *Brahman* and *acharanam;* together they translate as 'practice that directs us to the knowledge of *Brahman*'. A child of about eight is initiated into this stage, which promotes disciplines like celibacy, study and respect. The *upanayana* ceremony marks entry into this stage of life. In ancient times the child would be expected to live with his teacher to acquire education. He is expected to develop skills that will allow him to earn a living.

Relevance today: Gender attraction is a major distraction during the student stage of life and a celibate lifestyle is the best way to counter this challenge. The ideals of celibacy and showing respect for teachers may appear outdated, but modern educationalists are now beginning to recognise their true importance and are seeking to reinstall them into modern teaching methods.

The Householder is responsible for bearing the burden of all ~ *Grihastha*

The word *grihastha* derives from the Sanskrit word for 'house', *griham*. The second phase of life is that of the householder and usually begins after the individual has completed his studies. Entry into a householder's life is marked by the wedding ceremony, *vivah*. The individual is expected to earn a living, acquire wealth: *artha,* and fulfil his legitimate desires: *kama.* All these are to be carried out under the guidance of *dharma* or righteousness. The householder is expected to start a family and must provide financial support to the family and society.

Relevance today: The householder must look after the needs of *all* his family members including children and parents, and of other close relatives. In modern times the couple are only expected to look after their children while this ancient system insists that the couple look after their parents as well as distant family members. They are expected to provide for guests, and should contribute towards the welfare of their community and society. The householder, in this sense, provides financial support to the whole social structure. This is a pivotal stage in life dedicated to the service of others. This stage in life emphasises that religious life is not a matter of learning to *live with others* but learning to *live for others*. Sri Ramakrishna said, "If a householder does charity in a spirit of detachment, he makes great spiritual progress. It is God alone that he serves, God who dwells in all beings."

Grihastha
Caring for the family and the community

Time to withdraw from desires ~ *Vanaprastha*

The word *vanaprastha* derives from two Sanskrit words *vanam* meaning 'forest' and *prastha* implying 'going to'. Hence, the third *ashrama,* the *vanaprastha ashrama,* is the 'forest-dweller' stage of life. This expression may sound obscure, but means a life of retirement. The *ashrama* system was fully in operation thousands of years ago, many men and women, after fulfilling their duties in the *grihastha ashrama* retired to live in forests, away from worldly attachments. This third stage of life is therefore set aside for detachment from secular living, and for making spiritual progress. This age of retirement was around fifty, or according to some scriptures, "when the skin becomes wrinkled." The individual adopts an advisory role within the family and allows the next generation to take over the burden of running the household. 'The forest dweller' must spend time in meditation, contemplation and pilgrimage.

Vanaprastha
Time to retire from worldly affairs

Relevance today: The aim of this stage of life is detachment or withdrawal from worldly pursuits and more importantly, the withdrawal of the mind from all worldly *desires*. Most people these days "die in the saddle", without making any effort to progress spiritually. The teachings of *vanaprastha* are an important reminder to re-examine our priorities.

Sacrificing the trivial in order to attain the highest ~ *Sanyasa*

The *sanyasa ashrama* is the fourth and final phase in life and traditionally begins at the end of the *vanaprastha ashrama*. The lifestyle of a renunciate can however, be adopted at *any age* or *any stage in life* when the individual feels a strong urge for making spiritual progress. In earlier times, a *sanyasi,* a person in the *sanyasa ashrama*, would leave his home and family and become a monk. Traditionally, he does not keep any possessions with him except a small water vessel and a staff.

The word renunciation is often misunderstood. The monk is only renouncing 'less significant worldly goals' in order to attain a 'higher goal' i.e. God. The monk gives up his small family so that he can look upon the whole world as his family.

Relevance today: The two aims promoted at this stage of life are *moksha,* striving for liberation from the cycle of rebirth, and service to mankind. As *Swami Ramdas* said: "God realisation is not getting away from the world, but looking upon it as a manifestation of God and serving Him in all creatures and beings."

Sanyasa
Renounce the trivial in order to gain the highest ~ God

Breadth of vision

Rituals and Ceremonials

Rituals and ceremonials form an integral part of every religion. In this way, religion is given expression in the daily routine. Daily worship can be seen as an essential discipline that allows the individual to focus on God. Some ceremonials, for example rites of passage, bring families and communities together. In multi-faith societies, these occasions offer opportunities for people to learn about each other's faiths. Criticism can always be levelled at many rituals that they have become lifeless, mechanical or meaningless. All ritual should evolve to reflect the changing needs of society. If this is not done, they can sometimes become counter-productive. Hinduism offers great freedom in the way these rituals can be carried out but unfortunately in many cases this freedom is used as an excuse to abandon all rituals. Critics of religion could always argue that the money and time spent on all rituals is wasted and could have been better spent in caring for the needy.

Relevance of values promoted in the *Ashrama* system

Though the *ashrama* system is no longer practised, it offers deep insight into values that are still relevant. These values are better promoted through religious teachings than through secular teachings.

Respect

Promoting respect is an essential ingredient in any civilised society. Respect for the teacher facilitates better transmission of knowledge. Respect for other family members produces greater cohesion in the family. Respect for authority generates a more orderly society with better community cohesion.

Celibacy

Though celibacy appears old fashioned, Hinduism places great emphasis in promoting it to the young. It is well recognised that the greatest distraction in the student stage of life is sex. A promiscuous lifestyle results in low self-esteem and loss of personal dignity, while a celibate lifestyle results in a focused approach to life.

Live for others

Translating religion into practice is simply *learning to live for others*. This teaching arises naturally in religions, whereas the secular worldview emphasises *individuality* or living for oneself. The householder stage in life allows one to fulfil one's legitimate desires but this has to be done in a spirit of care and responsibility towards the rest of the family and community. In married life, this care translates as not asserting individuality, but learning to live for each other in a spirit of self-sacrifice. This simple religious teaching can prevent the breakdown of many marriages. Love and care should also be extended towards the elderly in the family. Why should the state look after the old? The idea of an extended family is to cater for the elderly within the family unit.

Withdrawal from desires

Hinduism is a pragmatic religion; it recognises that desires cannot be bottled up. Hence the householder in the *grihastha* stage in life, is allowed to fulfil his legitimate desires. However, it is also recognised that 'desires' have a habit of multiplying. A sense of maturity is encouraged in later stages of life. In the later stages of life one is expected to withdraw from desires. It is a great pity that modern Hindus have lost this art of withdrawing gracefully from desires.

Memory guide

Puja	Worship ceremony; acts as a daily reminder
Murti	An image of God worshipped in the shrine during *puja*
Pratima	Sanskrit term for an image; 'image that takes us closer to God'
Diva	A lamp that is lit during worship to represent transition from ignorance to illumination
Tilak	A mark on the forehead between the eyebrows to signify the individual's aspiration for spiritual awakening, gives a sense of belonging
Arti	A ceremony to welcome or invoke God, the focal activity of the *puja*
Prashad	Food offered to God at *puja* becomes sanctified and is distributed at the end of the ceremony. Holy food
Shikhar	An architectural design similar to a steeple; traditionally used in all temples as a reminder of pursuing lofty ideals
Garbha-Griha	The inner shrine where the central deities are housed
Darshan	To 'catch sight' of the deity
Brahmin	A priest who carries out rituals and ceremonials
Bhajans	Devotional songs and recitations praising God
Janmasthami	Birthday of Krishna at midnight
Ramanavami	Birthday of Rama at midday
Holi	A festival that announces the arrival of spring and commemorates a legendary story of a young boy *Prahlad* saved by *Vishnu*
Navaratri	A nine day festival signifying the arrival of autumn; celebrates the victory of the good over evil through a story of the Mother Goddess
Diwali	The popular Hindu festival at the start of winter; celebrates the night *Rama* returned from exile
Guru-purnima	Celebrating relationship between the *guru* and disciple
Yatra	A spiritual journey - a pilgrimage
Tirtha	Places of pilgrimage; where symbolically the individual can cross over from this world to the spiritual world
Varanasi	Place of pilgrimage - the abode of *Shiva* on the bank of the *Ganges*
Ayodhya	The birth place of *Rama* on the bank of *Saryu* in *Utter Pradesh*
Vrindavan	The place where *Krishna* sported as a child, near his birthplace *Mathura*
Samskara	Rite of passage; ritual performed to instil good impressions
Namakarana	One of the *samskaras*; the naming ceremony of the child
Upanayana	Sacred thread ceremony; getting closer to God; initiating entry into student stage of life around the age of eight
Vivah	Marriage ceremony marking entry into a householder's life
Panigrahana	The bride's father offers the hand of the bride to the groom
Sahadharmini	The wife is referred to as a companion in spiritual progress
Antima Kriya	The final *samskara*; cremation
Ashrama	The Hindu division of life into four stages; 'that which needs effort'
Dharma	Righteous living; guiding principle in the practice of religion
Artha	The accumulation of wealth; one of the aims of life
Kama	The satisfaction of legitimate desires; acceptable aim in life
Brahmacharya	The Student stage of life promoting: celibacy, study, and respect
Grihastha	The life of a householder; creating a family unit; looking after all
Vanaprastha	The 'forest-dweller's' life; age of withdrawal and retirement
Sanyasa	The life of renunciation; giving up trivial to gain the highest. The whole world is his family. Finding God through service to mankind

Chapter 6
RELIGION AND RATIONALITY

The distance between Belief and Proof
It is not only religions that ask us to believe in something, science does it all the time. Every hypothesis in science is a belief system. A scientist observes some patterns in the physical universe and in order to explain these, he offers a hypothesis or a belief system that fits the facts. The mature scientist never claims to have 'proved' anything, he simply offers a 'hypothesis' that best fits the facts. As we discover more and more patterns in the universe, our hypotheses continue to evolve to take into account of the new observations. None of these hypotheses can be called correct or absolute, but they offer the best explanation for the time being. If we do not start with a belief system (or a hypothesis) we can never make any progress in science.

Hindus believe the same method should be used in religion. Belief in God is a wonderful starting point or hypothesis in a religious journey, but we must not stop there. We must progress so that 'belief is replaced by some kind of proof.' And the proof of God can only come with first hand experience of God. The only way we 'prove' God is by experiencing Him for ourselves; this is the bold conclusion of the Hindu philosophy.

Rationality in Religion
Like *Adi Shankara* (788-820), who emphasised the importance of rationality in religion, Vivekananda (1863-1902) has re-emphasised the role of rationality in religion. He taught that "Religions may ask us to believe in transcendent truths but never irrational ones. Without adhering to the standard of rationality, religions degenerate into a mass of superstitions".

Shruti, Yukti and *Swanubhuti*
Study in any field, including religions, follows the same procedure: Start with a hypothesis, then take it to its rational conclusion and finally validate this conclusion through first hand experience. The term *shruti* means taking guidance from the earlier authoritative texts or theories, the term *yukti* means using rationality to understand, interpret and take these teachings to their logical conclusion. The term *swanubhuti* means that the understanding thus derived, is only valid if it can be tested experimentally. Modern science follows the same dictum that Hinduism has prescribed for spiritual progress. First, religious beliefs should be tested by the standard of reason. Even then, they are not accepted as valid, unless they can be experienced first hand. Just as a hypothesis in science is considered to be valid only if it can be demonstrated by experiment, belief in God is only acceptable if God can be experienced first hand. This is a far more stringent requirement than the requirement of science, as the experiment has to be conducted first hand.

Adi Shankara
Promoted rationality as a necessary tool for spiritual progress

69

God cannot just be a matter of belief ~ nor can He be a by-product of our mental gymnastics. He is a matter of experience

Hindus do not encourage the idea that God should just be a matter of belief, but insist that God has to be a matter of first hand experience. Rationality is emphasised as like an abrasive, it removes inconsistencies in our worldview. Though it may not be able to capture God in its framework, it helps to remove the dross that obscures our experience of God.

Limits of rationality

The reason why rationality cannot capture God (or give conclusive evidence of God) is because it is after all only a subset of our minds; thus if it had the power to capture God, then our minds become as big or bigger than God. This in turn would mean that God is not truly 'Ultimate', which contradicts the definition of God. Even though rationality is seen as a powerful tool, in the final instance, it has to fail in proving the existence of God. If this is not the case, God becomes a subset of our mental faculty. The only way God can be proved is by first hand experience.

Metaphor to explain the role of rationality in religion

Suppose we find ourselves locked in a darkened room and are keen to behold the brilliant sunlight outside the room. And suppose the only tool we have is a small torch with a weak battery. Should we use the torch or switch it off, as it is so weak? The answer is, we have to use the torch, as it is the best thing we have in order to search for the door and the door handle that allows escape from the dark room. Once we open the door, there is no further need for the torch: we do not have to shine the torch on the sun to prove that it exists.

In the same manner, we grope for God in our state of ignorance. The best tool we have is our rational faculty. Though this faculty is limited, it is the best thing we have for making spiritual progress. This faculty allows us to make sense of the world we live in and look for handles to turn. By turning a handle we can escape our state of ignorance and are able to behold the sun (God). Only after we have done this, does rationality become redundant. Just as the torch does not conjure up the sun, rationality does not conjure up God, but helps us to remove the ignorance that stops us from beholding God.

The three attitudes to religion	
Theists say:	there is God, a personality that governs everything
Atheists say:	there is NO God as there is no proof of God
Agnostics say:	we cannot prove or disprove God

1.   Theism ~ there is God

The word theism is taken from the Greek word *theos,* meaning God. Monotheists are people who believe in a creator God. They think of God as a personality who is omnipotent (all powerful), omniscient (all knowing), omnipresent (present everywhere), eternal everlasting and all loving. He is also described as Transcendent (meaning not of this world) and Immanent (meaning inherent in everything). Most Hindu devotees adopt the attitude of a monotheist, but then Hindu philosophy points out that this attitude is the starting point in a spiritual journey, which has to end with first hand experience of God.

2.   Atheism ~ there is NO God

This is a belief system that does not accept the existence of God. An atheist claims that there is NO God. A fundamental problem for the atheist is the question: How can we prove that something *does not* exist? It is far more difficult to prove that something does *not* exist than to prove that something *does* exist. Nevertheless, atheists are people who are convinced that the concept of God can be explained *away* in rational terms. The way they wish to win their argument is by showing *inconsistencies* in the theistic explanations of God. That, in their view, is proof enough that God does not exist.

Bertrand Russell
Mathematician & Philosopher

- **Humanists** are atheists who challenge all religions, believing them to be false and harmful to society. According to them, the goal of life is to make the most of what we have here, as there is no hereafter. They promote the idea that we have to organise ourselves so that we can all live fruitful and enjoyable lives.

Hindu philosophy agrees with the Humanists that mankind is very important, but disagrees with them when they insist that man is just a 'sophisticated lump of matter'. Hindus argue that if we are nothing more than 'matter', then it does not make any sense whether we, as 'lumps of matter', suffer or are happy, as such words have no meaning for lumps of matter. Happiness and unhappiness are *non-material* subjective phenomena. Unless there is more to us than 'matter', pursuing happiness becomes pointless too. Hindus therefore promote **spiritual humanism,** which affirms that the essential nature of man is spirit ~*Atman*.

David Hume
Scottish philosopher

3.   Agnosticism ~ we can neither prove nor disprove God. Hindus agree

Agnostic is a word derived from the Greek root *gno,* which in turn comes from the Sanskrit *jnana,* meaning 'to know'. The prefix 'A' was added to this term by Thomas Huxley (1825-1895) to mean *not knowable.* Agnostics claim that they cannot say conclusively that God exists, nor can they say that he does not exist. One may be surprised to learn that Hindu philosophy agrees with this stand. Hindus argue, "How can it be possible to prove the existence of God? What faculty do we possess that has the same validity as God, that it can offer credence to God? If we had any such faculty, then that faculty, by definition, would be of the same calibre as God. But then we end up with two ultimates! That is a contradiction in terms, hence the Hindu philosophy accepts an agnostic stance saying "God cannot be proved or disproved through *rational enquiry.*"

Bearing the Hindu pre-requisite, that it *cannot* be possible to prove God through any form of elaborate rational gymnastics, we explore various arguments put forward (mainly by Christian theologians) as 'proof of the existence of God.'

Thomas Huxley
Coined the term A-gnostic
(God is not knowable)

"Reasonable" arguments offered as proof of the existence of God.

Design theory ~ is God really a good designer?
The observed universe is so intricate, so well balanced and awe-inspiring, that it encourages the idea, that behind this intricate design, there must be a *designer God.* William Paley, an eighteenth century theologian exemplified this idea as a 'design' argument for the proof of God. He explained that the discovery of a watch and the examination of its intricacies, suggests the existence of a watchmaker. Similarly, the elaborate universe implies the existence of an intelligent designer: God.

Criticisms:

- **Bad designer:** The first objection to this theory is that if God designed everything, then he is not a very good designer. When we look around we find so many faults with the universe; so many living things are poorly designed with all sorts of deficiencies, like poor eyesight etc. so this would mean that either God is not so perfect or that he did not design the universe. Either way this theory is seen as unsatisfactory.

- **Just a raw fact of nature:** The famous mathematician and philosopher Bertrand Russell (1872-1970) refutes this argument. He believes that this intricate universe is not proof enough for the existence of God, but merely a *raw fact* of nature.

- **Weak analogy:** Another critic of this argument is the Scottish philosopher David Hume, (1711-1776) who does not believe that the creation of a watch is similar to the creation of the universe. He calls this comparison a 'weak analogy', as the clock is nowhere similar to the totality of the universe.

- **Evolution:** The 'design and causation' argument as proof of God has been dealt a severe blow by the contemporary evolutionary biologist Richard Dawkins. He believes that the mystery of life and its elaborate workings can be explained by Darwin's theory of evolution based on natural selection and random genetic mutations without reference to God.

Charles Darwin
Formulated the theory of Evolution

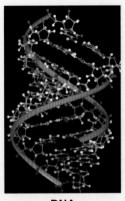

DNA
the secret of life wound up in a strand

Hindu philosophy agrees with the conclusion of these skeptics: The 'design' argument does not offer conclusive evidence of God.

Everything has a cause; the universe must have a cause ~ so is that God?

Some theologians suggest that someone must have created the universe, and *that* someone must be God. Everything requires a cause, so there must be a 'first cause' that produced this universe. That first cause must be God. Even though the theory sounds plausible, it is flawed.

Criticisms:

- **So who created God?** If *everything* requires a cause, then God too must have a cause and that something else must have been caused by something else, and so on. Either everything (this includes God) must have a cause or we have to stop using *causality* to prove God!

- **The Big Bang:** Modern cosmology offers a plausible explanation as to how the universe may have come into existence about fifteen billion years ago through a Big Bang without reference to a creator God. Some Christian theologians suggest that even Big Bang must have a cause and that cause is God. Hindus disagree, they argue that 'causation' too came into being together with space and time at the time of the big bang hence 'who caused the big bang' is an irrelevant question and thus there is no need for a creator God.

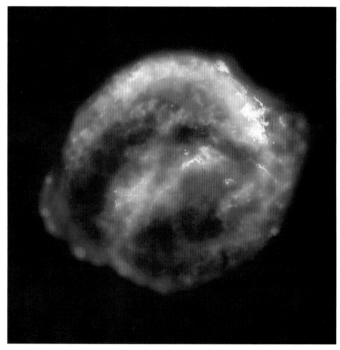

Big Bang
The start of another cycle of creation (*kalpa*)

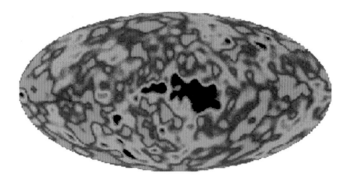

Big Bang Radiation
The background radiation is still visible

God is mysterious ~ 'not a good idea' say Hindus.

Fascination with the occult or mysterious is perhaps one of the reasons why some people are drawn to believe in God.

Criticism:

This encourages superstitions: The secretive and mystical approach may be appealing to some but is discouraged in Hinduism, as it fosters superstition, weakness and fear. All mysterious phenomena should be challenged and examined rationally rather than be accepted as proof of something supernatural.

Only God can do magic ~ Are miracles a proof of God?

Another argument offered as proof of God is that of miracles. Some people think that miracles are the best proof of God's existence.

- **Miracles are just natural phenomena not yet understood:** Many Hindus do not like the idea of miracles. Many natural phenomena, for example 'eclipses' were considered to be miraculous in ancient times, but now they can be explained away through astronomy. In the same way, many events that are classed as miracles at present may be explained away in rational terms without reference to God in the future. We may discover for example, that miraculous cures of patients suffering from terminal illnesses may have come about by the unconscious use of our mental energies in wishing a patient better, rather than by some supernatural agency engaging in producing a miraculous cure. Such events are classed as 'miraculous cures.' However, Hindus would *also* accept that if there is a God who has created the laws of nature, then He certainly would have the power to bend these laws if he chose to do so. Though it would be impossible to comprehend how and why He would do such things.

A Miracle
Does God intervene in such a manner?

Criticisms of Miracles as proof of God

- **God has lost control:** If God is forced to keep intervening in this manner, then it means that his created universe keeps getting out of his control and he has to keep tweaking the system suggesting that he is not in complete control of his creation.
- **God is partial:** Why should he intervene to help the believers? He should intervene even more for the unbelievers as they need his help even more.
- **Unreliable Witnesses:** Sceptics like David Hume suggest pointedly that witnesses to miracles are unreliable witnesses. These people are mostly uneducated and are predisposed to believe in miracles, hence their testimony is invalid. People see what they want to see!

So many wonderful buildings ~ does this mean that God exists?

The fact that we see so many places of worship like temples, mosques, churches and synagogues all over the world may be offered as proof of God. Why should there be so many elaborate, wonderful structures in the world, if there is no God? How can so many people be inspired to build such beautiful structures over so many thousands of years, if there is no God? This argument may satisfy some people but many would disagree.

- **Criticism: Does Disney world mean Mickey Mouse is for real?** The first criticism of the above argument can be simply put as: "Disney world has many elaborate and beautiful structures, does this prove that Mickey Mouse exists?" The fact that we build structures to express our beliefs does not mean that our beliefs are justified.

- **Which God is for real?** All these structures depict different Gods, so either one religion is right and all others are wrong, or more likely all are wrong. This is a strong argument used against religions called: "Playing one religion against another."

Brought up to believe in God ~ a good start but not good enough.
Being brought up in a religious family certainly nurtures faith in God. This belief should not be an end in itself, but should be utilised as a stepping stone towards making spiritual progress and discovering God for oneself. As the saying suggests "it is good to be born in a church but it is not good to die in one", meaning that belief is a good starting point in a religious journey but it should not be the end. It is emphasised by Hindus that if one person in the history of mankind has been able to experience God, and if God is a universal phenomenon, then it must be possible for every human being to experience God first hand. The aim of life, according to Vivekananda, is not just to believe in God, but to realise God.

Revelation as proof of God?
Revelation is considered by many religions as the best proof of God. Revelation can be classed broadly into three categories:

Revelation in scriptures ~ Is God caught between the pages of a book?
Many claim that scriptural writings are valid proof of God, as they are written records and as such provide *solid* proof of God! Hindus too claim that their scriptures of authority, the Vedas are revealed scriptures, but then these scriptures boldly claim that God is not captured in its folds. At best such scriptures offer a *perception* of God but never God himself.

The Self (God) cannot be attained by the study of the Vedas nor by intellectual gymnastics, nor by listening to discourses.... *Kathopanishad 1.II.23*

Revelation by prophets
Devotees may claim that the best proof of God is the spiritual experience of their prophets.

- **Criticism: The experience may be brain malfunction:** Claims of revelation, with visions of light or burning bushes or angels, may be argued to be just hallucination due to brain malfunction.

- **We have to experience God:** Hindus would agree that the experiences of the prophets are good guidelines, but suggest that if prophets were able to experience God, then we should take our inspiration from them to experience God for ourselves. If God is so wonderful, why should we just believe in Him and sit back? We should make an effort to experience him here and now.

Revelation the Hindu way ~ first hand experience of God is the *only* way
Hindus say it is all very good that a scripture or a prophet declares the existence of God, but that can only take us so far. We should take encouragement from such revelations and make efforts to experience God for ourselves, as this is the only definitive proof of the existence of God.

Tranquillity of Mind
allows us to experience God as our innermost nature

The Self (God) is subtler than the subtlest, greater than the greatest, and is seated in the heart of every creature. One who is free of desires, sees the glory of the Self through the tranquillity of the mind and senses and becomes absolved from grief. *Kathopanishad 1.II.20*

"Reasonable" proofs of the non-existence of God ~ The challenge to Religions
Various theological explanations have been offered to support mankind's belief in God. However, some of the brightest minds are not satisfied with such explanations. They consider the idea of God as a 'super-personality responsible for creating and looking after the world', irrational.

Challenges from Science

- **The Big Bang:** Modern cosmological theories are now considered to be a more rational, scientific explanation for creation. It is believed that the whole creation came into being about fifteen billion years ago with the 'Big Bang'. Our earth was formed about four and a half billion years ago. Hindus agree with the idea of cyclic creation and destruction. Time is viewed as cyclic, explained through the idea of *kalpa.*

- **Evolution:** The theory of evolution was promoted by a biologist called Charles Darwin (1809-1882). The theory says that natural selection is responsible for the evolution of mankind from single celled living organisms that may have come into being about four billion years ago. The theory challenges the Abrahamic notions of God creating the universe in six days, or God creating vegetation and animals on specific days. God creating the first man as Adam about four thousand years ago, is strongly refuted by evolutionary biologists. Some theologians respond by saying that Biblical stories should be treated as allegoric and not literal truths, while other theologians claim that the world was created in 4004 BC, but the devil is making mischief by deluding us into thinking it is billions of years old! Hindus agree with the theory of evolution but suggest that genetic mutations are not random, but a directed process.

Do religions provide the best basis for ethics and morality?
The claim that religions provide the best basis for moral codes is refuted by social science.

- Religions have a habit of promoting rules of ethics and morality that are set in stone. Many of these rules cannot be altered nor adapted to address changing circumstances, hence they are not the best codes of conduct for society, is the argument put forward by social scientists. They claim that the rules of morality that social sciences offer are far more flexible and reflect the changing needs of society.

- Hinduism would agree and take this argument forward by saying that no code of conduct should be set in stone. Every code is contextual and must change when the circumstances change. The laws of morality have to evolve in order to reflect the changing needs of society. Hence the law-books of Hinduism, like the *Manusmriti,* came with a sale-by-date. This does *not* mean that as nothing is fixed, '*anything goes*'. This is called **relativism.** Hinduism disagrees with relativism by saying that although the rules of society have to be flexible, they are *still binding in each situation.*

- Hindus refute the claim that social sciences are better than religions at promoting moral values. They claim that morality is given a firmer footing through religious teachings based on spiritual findings than through social engineering. For example the teaching of *Advaita Vedanta* gives the best reason why we should help and not harm other living things. "Because at the spiritual level we are the same, so we hurt ourselves when we hurt others!" is a more logical explanation offered as to why we should be moral. At best, social science can teach us how to live *with* others. Religion on the other hand teaches us how to live *for* others.

Religion explained away as a psychological or social phenomenon
Psychologists such as Sigmund Freud (1856-1939) suggests that belief in God is an unconscious ploy used by mankind to gain comfort during times of distress or to overcome the fear of death.

- Hindus disagree: the fact that belief in God helps us to face such issues does not *necessarily* prove that God *does not* exist. In fact, it suggests the opposite, the possibility that He *does* exist, as in His name such issues are being resolved.

Social scientists like Emile Durkheim argue that the idea of God is an unconscious ploy used by societies to exercise control over the thoughts and behaviour of the individuals.

- Hindus disagree: the teachings of prophets of most religions have almost always *opposed* many of the social conventions of the time. So how can religious teachings be explained away as unconscious ploys of these societies?

Tackling the problem of suffering
The principle reason for disbelief in an almighty and compassionate God is evidence of the abundance of suffering of all living things, including mankind. Belief in the existence of an all-merciful, all-powerful and all knowing God is in direct contradiction to the suffering we see all around us.

No Devil in Hinduism
One response by the Abrahamic religions is that God is good and almighty and does not want us to suffer, but there is another mighty personality called the Devil who spoils things for mankind, thus causing suffering.

- **God should eliminate the devil:** Common sense would suggest that if God is *almighty*, it should be easy for him to eliminate the Devil and free mankind from suffering.

The Freewill defence ~ One fudge to tackle another fudge
To overcome the difficulty of explaining away suffering, some theologians like St. Augustine saw fit to put the blame on mankind, hence absolving God of any responsibility for causing suffering. This is called the freewill defence. The theory goes: God gave mankind 'freedom of choice', but mankind chose poorly and hence suffers. The wrongdoings of mankind, like murder, fighting, wars etc. are defined as **'moral evil'** and blamed for suffering. This defence is not satisfactory. It is one fudge (the idea of freewill itself is non-sense. How can 'will' be free? It is always *someone's* will hence it is tied to that individual!) used to tackle another fudge (the difficulty of explaining suffering).

Criticisms:
- As God is *all knowing,* he should have *known* that mankind will choose poorly, and should not have trusted mankind with freewill.

- Then there is also the question of **'natural evil'** i.e. natural disasters such as famines, drought, earthquakes etc. How can mankind's freewill be blamed for such events? No answer is offered.

- 'God is testing us through suffering' or 'wants us to become strong through suffering' are pretty weak excuses offered to save this theory. The end cannot justify the means. All such arguments show God in poor light.

Hindu response: Let us begin by analysing what suffering is and then let us attempt to reconcile this with the concept of God as a personality and as a principle.

First analyse what suffering is, say the Hindus

Suffering is *always* subjective
It is important to recognise that suffering is always subjective; it is always *someone's* suffering. The resolution to the question of suffering can only come by *first* incorporating the idea of a 'subject' into the equation.

- **Physical suffering ~ the tax we pay for having a body**
  Suffering is always *'someone's* suffering, it is a subjective phenomenon. Hindus classify human suffering as either physical, mental or spiritual. Many forms of physical suffering are just survival mechanisms of the body and are vital for self-preservation. For example, putting a hand in fire results in physical pain. It is this pain that makes us pull our hand away from the fire to prevent further harm. The development of such sensitivities is essential for human sustenance, hence this form of suffering is inherent in the way living things function. Therefore blame cannot be laid on an unmerciful God or a spiteful Devil. Such suffering is a vital survival mechanism for the body.

Because the spirit is trying to manifest in a physical body, such suffering is inevitable. Other unavoidable forms of physical suffering are disease, old age and death, which according to Sri Ramakrishna are the "taxes we pay for having a body". The fact that we all possess a body means that physical suffering is inevitable. Why God set up such a scheme of things, we do not know.

- **Mental suffering is due to unfulfilled desires**
  Mental suffering according to Hinduism , is caused by unfulfilled desires. Desires spring up as we feel we are lacking in something. Mental suffering *is* avoidable. Vivekananda says, "We must learn to live like a master and not a servant. As long as we expect something from the world we expose ourselves to suffering". We must desire nothing from the world, but learn to be satisfied within ourselves. In stark contrast, the modern commercial world functions by 'promoting desires.' The sole function of all advertisements is to make us feel that we are lacking something. Stoking up the flames of desires that can never be fulfilled results in stress and frustration. This is a modern disease mankind has inflicted upon itself.

- **Spiritual suffering ~ yearning for freedom**
  Spiritual suffering is the yearning of the heart for freedom from *all* bondage. The reason for spiritual suffering is ignorance of our true nature, the *Atman*. We are used to thinking that we are just the 'mind and body complex', and hence chase after the needs of the mind and body. Hinduism teaches that we are essentially not the mind and body complex. Recognising ourselves as the witness and not as what is being witnessed, is the only way of ending spiritual suffering. *Swami Ramdas* states that "true freedom and happiness is an inner state which you acquire when you are in tune with God who dwells within you". True happiness does not come through the frenzied activities we engage in, but comes naturally through mental tranquility.

Why such an unfair set-up? "We really don't know" say the Hindus
So far, we have not answered the question of why God created a world where suffering is inevitable. Hindus bluntly say that they *do not* possess the answer to this pointed question. They simply say that *there is* God and *there is* suffering; and somehow we have to reconcile the two.

Desires are the cause of mental suffering

Desires for sense objects come from attachment to sense objects, and anger arises from unfulfilled desires, delusion comes from such activities, and the mind becomes bewildered thus losing the sense of reasoning. With the loss of reasoning comes complete ruin

Bhagavad Gita 2.61-63

One who abandons all desires and becomes free from longing and feeling of me and mine, attains peace

Bhagavad Gita 2.71

Tackling the issue of suffering becomes a major Indian Religion
There is a false notion that Hindus blame the law of *karma* for suffering. The law of *karma* is purely a law of cause and effect, a transmitting mechanism and as such can be blamed for anything and everything under the sun. Hence this is not the answer that Hindus offer to explain suffering. Hindus have thought very hard about this problem. One of the offshoots of Hinduism is Buddhism. This religion focuses solely on the issue of suffering and how to overcome it without reference to God.

The Problem of Suffering
Buddha discovers that disease, old-age and death are inevitable

How to live with suffering?
Hindus have adopted two approaches that allow them to *live* with suffering.

- **1. Response from Hindus who believe in God as a personality ~ The *Dvaita* way of handling suffering**
  Dvaita philosophy, which believes that God and mankind are separate, teaches that one must accept both pain and pleasure as the 'play' or **leela** of God. By doing this, one is not able to get rid of pain, but can view it differently. God's play or *leela,* can only be interesting if there are both laughter and tears, hence this game devised by God contains pleasure as well as suffering. This does not resolve the problem of suffering, but offers an attitude to handle suffering. A true devotee will accept the harshest suffering as the play of God. Let us illustrate this with a story.

Leela ~ God's Play ~ He plays through us

A holy man was walking through a dense forest where he was attacked by thieves. When the thieves discovered that he had no belongings worth stealing, they beat him up and threw him in a ditch. After a while, some people passing by saw the holy man in the ditch and pulled him out. After tending to his wounds, one of them started pouring milk down his throat and asked, "Who did this to you?" The holy man replied that it is the same *One* who beat him up and threw him in the ditch, who is now pouring milk down his throat.

A true devotee treats whatever comes his way, pleasure or the harshest pain, as the *play* of God. Frequently this play is very severe indeed. The redeeming feature of this approach is that it emphasises that it is God alone who is playing all these different roles; it is He alone who is crying and laughing and it is He alone who is inflicting this play on Himself.

- **2. Response from Hindus who believe in God as a principle ~ The *Advaita* response**
  Advaita philosophy, which identifies our essential nature with God, views the issue of suffering differently. It says that both pleasure and pain are relative phenomena; we cannot have one without the other. To suggest that we can live in heaven where we will experience pleasure forever is naive. (We may like chocolate cake, but if we were asked to eat chocolate cake forever, we would soon find it repulsive). So to think that we can live in a state of pleasure alone is baby's prattle. Pleasure and pain are like two sides of the same coin. We cannot have one without the other. Hindus say that the problem is not *how* to remove pain, but *how to rise above* or transcend *both* pleasure and pain. The way to do this is to realise that we are not the mind or the body. We are essentially something beyond that.

Maya: Advaitic teachings tackle the problem of suffering through the concept of *maya*: both pleasure and pain are seen as bondage. The goal of spiritual progress is to transcend both pleasure and pain as they are subsidiary to our natural state of *ananda* or 'bliss'. Bliss is our real nature. As Vivekananda states: "What we want is neither happiness nor misery. Both make us forget our true nature; both are chains, one of iron, another gold; behind both is the *Atman*." The aim of *Advaita Vedanta* is to break these shackles and obtain freedom, *kaivalya*. We have to transcend pleasure and pain and gain bliss by identifying ourselves with God.

At best, Hinduism teaches us how to live *with* suffering. The resolution *to* suffering only comes with God experience
Both of these approaches do not dissolve the suffering of mankind, but offer ways of handling it. Suffering is seen as a crucial prod that leads mankind to search for God. It is only when we become identified with God, that suffering ends, and this is the conclusion of Hindu philosophy. This perhaps is the only redeeming aspect to suffering - it forces us to find God.

Ramakrishna
explains: Identifying ourselves with God is the only way to escape suffering

Breadth of vision

The Role of rationality

"Religious truths may be transcendent but never irrational", says Vivekananda. "Why religions are not expected to conform to the standard of reason, no one knows. Religion without rationality turns into an incongruent mass of superstitions, and rationality without religion turns into dry rhetoric. Reconciling religion with rationality is essential, otherwise religions are seen as irrelevant for modern times.

God cannot be proved or disproved

One of the key ideas to come out of Hindu philosophy is that God cannot be proved or disproved. He is destined to remain crucially invisible, and this is not seen as a weakness. In fact this is seen as an essential philosophic condition to maintain the potency of God. Hindu philosophy smiles at the futile mental gymnastics carried out by Christian theologians to prove the existence of God, and the equally futile gymnastics carried out by the modern psychologists and social scientists to disprove God.

So how do we validate God?

The only entity that can pass judgement about God has to be of equal calibre to God and fortunately for us that entity is our own essential nature (*Atman*). Because we are essentially expressions of the same God, it becomes possible to verify God in the most personal and intense manner. Hence God cannot be a matter of belief, but has to be a matter of 'realisation' in Hinduism. The experience of God is considered to be far more intense, dynamic and life altering than anything our minds can experience. Rationality would agree that this has to be the case, else God becomes a figment of our mental realm.

Have we explained God away?

The arrogant stance of modern materialists that they can explain away everything in terms of matter is in serious jeopardy with the recent findings of modern Physics. These findings clearly indicate that matter is not the primary building block of the universe, it is a secondary phenomenon! The next volume in this series examines the findings of Quantum Mechanics that suggest a spiritual underpinning to the physical universe. It is not the prophets of the past but the science of today that holds the key of leading mankind to spirituality.

Memory guide

Shankara	8th Century Hindu philosopher who emphasised rationality
Design Argument	The universe is so well balanced and intricate that a designer God must be responsible for creating it
Mandir	A Hindu temple; considered the earthly home of God
Atheism	The belief that there is no God; belief in disbelief
Agnosticism	Inability to confirm if God exists or not
Humanists	Atheists who think that religions are wrong and harmful to society
Natural Selection	The favouring of a particular species for survival based on its skills to adapt to the changing environment
William Paley	An 18th Century theologian who promoted the idea of a designer God
Bertrand Russell	A mathematician and philosopher who refuted the idea of God
David Hume	A critic of the 'design, causation and miracle' arguments for God
Richard Dawkins	A contemporary proponent of the theory of evolution
Charles Darwin	Biologist who promoted the theory of evolution over theory of creation
Revelation	Considered by many to be proof of God; can be seen as a way of life, through scriptures or through prophets
Thomas Huxley	An agnostic who is famous for coining the term a-gnostic
Sigmund Freud	Suggested that God is a psychological defence mechanism used by mankind to overcome distress and fear of death
Emile Durkheim	Social scientist who claims that the idea of God is an unconscious ploy of society to exercise control over the thoughts and behaviour of its members
Natural Evil	Natural calamities such as drought, earthquake, flood, bereavement
Moral Evil	Man-made suffering like wars, crime, marriage breakdown
Physical suffering	The inevitable bodily pain, such as disease, old age and death
Mental suffering	The result of desires; causing frustration, depression and stress
Spiritual suffering	The yearning of the heart for freedom and enlightenment
Leela	The 'play' of God; response to explain human suffering in *Dvaita Vedanta*
Maya	A concept adopted by *Advaita Vedantic* philosophy to explain human suffering; both pleasure and pain are bondage to be transcended. How is the spirit caught up in this? Through *maya*
Ananda	Bliss; a transcendental state beyond pleasure and pain
Kaivalya	Spiritual freedom; one without a second

EXTRA NOTES:

Chapter 7
LIFE AND DEATH

Is there any proof that something survives after death?

Near Death Experiences: One of the major criticisms of the belief in life after death is that there is no scientific evidence to back up this idea. However, recent research in the occurrence of 'Near Death Experiences' or 'NDE' reveals that individuals who come close to death, or have been temporarily declared clinically dead, report strange experiences suggestive of life after the death. Many of them report that they feel as if they have left their bodies and are hovering above them; in some cases they see and hear people talking at their deathbed. They state that they experience a sense of well being and freedom despite having no link with their bodies. Many of them report seeing a tunnel of light. At the end of the tunnel, they come into contact with their dead relatives. Sometimes these relatives ask them to return to their physical bodies.

- **It is just the lack of oxygen to the brain:** Some neuroscientists offer an alternative explanation to such experiences. They say that as the individual approaches death, the lack of oxygen reaching his brain creates hallucinations and sensations of floating out of the body, seeing a white light etc. These scientists claim that it is understandable that as the individual faces imminent death his mind would conjure up images of dead relatives. Hence they argue that NDE is not valid proof of life after death.

- **Seeing and hearing without the use of the body:** Near death experiences have not been fully explained away by such arguments. For example, there are many cases where the patients are declared brain dead, and yet after a few minutes they recover and recall actual conversations or events that took place in the operating theatre after they had been declared clinically dead. If there was no brain activity during this period, how could they hear or see? This is not an isolated phenomenon, and so far, science has not provided a reasonable explanation.

- **Why not conjure up images of _living_ relatives?** Another interesting aspect to this research is that even though the patients may be feeling extremely distressed during their near death experiences, they _never_ conjure up images of their _living_ relatives. Surely at such times, in some of these cases, the patients should conjure up images of the people whom they love and who are still alive. Surprisingly the near death experiences only conjure up images of people who have passed away. How could this be? No reasonable explanation has been offered so far.

- **Biological impossibility:** In some cases, patients have been declared clinically brain dead for such long periods of time that their recovery cannot be adequately explained in biological terms.

NDE makes the patients turn to spirituality: The feeling of wellbeing, warmth and love felt by all patients who undergo near death experiences, is indicative of possible life after death. The fact that a person somehow feels 'better' even though he is no longer linked with his body suggests that there is more to us than our bodies. In many cases patients who have undergone near death experiences become greatly changed. Many become spiritually inclined after such an experience, suggesting that the experiences are not hallucinations but very powerful and life-altering events.

Three views on life after death

Life after death	Atheists say we only have one life
	Abrahamic religions say we have two lives
	Indian religions say we have innumerable lives

1. We live only once ~ The Atheistic and Humanist view

Atheists and Humanists believe that there is only one life, the one that we have at the moment; the idea of life after death is just wishful thinking. It is best not to bother with such ideas but to concentrate on the life we have now and make the most of it.

The danger of adopting this attitude is that it may encourage reckless behaviour. Since this is the only life, we may be encouraged to be ruthless to achieve our goals at the expense of others' interests. However, the endearing aspect of this viewpoint is that it emphasises the importance of *this* life. Every moment becomes precious and should not be wasted. Life before death is given more importance than life after death.

2. We have only two lives ~ the Abrahamic view

Religions such as Christianity and Islam believe that we all have two lives: our present life and an eternal life in heaven or hell. They believe that after we die, we await the day of judgement when we are resurrected, (brought back to life) to be judged. If we have been good in this life, then we are rewarded and sent to heaven where we experience eternal pleasure. On the other hand if we have been bad, then we are sent to hell to be tortured forever.

Consequences of believing in the Abrahamic view

- **Pleasure without pain:** The belief that one can exist in heaven in a state of eternal pleasure is a misnomer. Pleasure and pain are like two sides of the same coin; they define each other. We cannot have one without the other. So the idea of eternal pleasure without pain is philosophically unsound.

- **Risk/Reward ratio is unjust:** Being offered infinite reward for finite good done in one life, or being subjected to infinite torture for finite bad action carried out in one lifetime cannot be justified. How can a merciful God allow anyone to be subjected to eternal torment?

- **Redeeming feature:** The reason why a belief with such a skewed risk/reward ratio may have been introduced into these religions, could be to keep the faithful well and truly focused on living a religious life.

3. We have innumerable lives ~ the Hindu, Buddhist, Jain & Sikh view

The theory of reincarnation is one of the key beliefs in all Indian religions. It states that all individuals participate in a cycle of birth and death. After we die, we are reborn in another body. The cycle continues until we find God, or as some Hindus would say, we identify ourselves with God. The idea of reincarnation was popular in the West until the 'Christian Council' declared the theory of reincarnation anathema (abhorrent) in 553AD. Since that time, the theory of reincarnation has not been accepted in the West; even though the belief was prevalent with the ancient Greek thinkers like Pythagoras, Plato and Socrates.

- **Why don't we remember our past lives?** The greatest criticism laid against this theory is that it sounds too preposterous. If we have lived many times in the past, why don't we remember any of our past lives? In response Hindus say that the transition from one life to another is an extremely traumatic experience. In order not to relive that pain, the mind blocks out the memory of previous lives. The mind acts as a defence mechanism blocking out knowledge of previous lives, else the memory of earlier lives with all the people we have loved and left behind would overwhelm us.

- **Is there hard evidence of reincarnation?** Professor Ian Stevenson of Virginia University in the USA has carried out a great deal of research on the theory of reincarnation. He has recorded thousands of cases of children from all around the world, who have been able to provide detailed accounts of their previous lives. In many cases a rigorous verification of these accounts has been possible. This evidence is not based on conjecture but on hard evidence. Professor Stevenson concludes that these facts can best be explained through the theory of reincarnation.

- **Measured rewards for measured risks:** One of the endearing aspects of the theory of reincarnation is that it offers measured rewards for measured risks we take. The individual gets what he deserves. The Hindu law of *karma* states that everything we do, will produce consequences that we must endure in this life or the next. Therefore, all the good work we may have done in this life does not go to waste when we die; it comes to fruition in our future life or lives.

- **Phobias explained:** The theory of reincarnation provides a wonderful explanation as to why people suffer from phobias (irrational fears). The theory suggests that the reason why, for example, a person may be afraid of heights may be because, in one of his previous lives, he could have died by falling from a great height. That fear remains in the psyche of that person and manifests as a phobia in his next life.

- **Geniuses:** The theory also explains why we have geniuses. It suggests that over many lifetimes, an individual may have worked hard to develop certain skills, for example in music. These skills become ingrained into the psyche of that person and reveal themselves at an early age when they are reborn. The classic example is that of Mozart who started composing operas at the age of 7!

Mozart

- **Gays:** The theory also gives an interesting insight into why some people may be homosexual (See Chapter 8). It suggests the possibility of a person switching genders from one life to another. Suppose a person who has been a female for many lives then switches gender. Although she may be in a male body, she still has a female personality (from her previous lives as a female). Thus in this life, that person, though in a male body, continues to be attracted to other males.

The Cycle of rebirth:
The Theory of reincarnation. As we discard old clothes for new ones,
we discard worn out bodies to take on new ones

Issue of Abortion

All life is Sacred ~ but when does life begin?
Hindus believe that life begins at the moment of conception, hence abortion at any stage of pregnancy would be morally wrong. Perhaps the only circumstance when abortion may be acceptable is if the mother's life is threatened. In such a difficult situation, there is no clear injunction as to whose life is more valuable, and the decision would be left to the family as to which life should be saved. The 1967 Abortion Act of the British Legislation states that "if the mother's life or health or if the baby's life or health is jeopardised, then pregnancy can be terminated". Even if conception has taken place through rape, or if

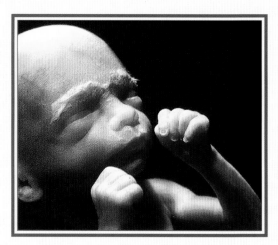

A foetus at 24 weeks in the womb

the unborn child is diagnosed to have a serious disability, life is considered sacred, and should not be terminated. However, the Hindu law of *karma* would give freedom to abort a baby if it is absolutely clear that the baby is in severe pain and has no hope of survival. Prolonging the suffering of a living thing when there is absolutely no chance of survival would be viewed as morally wrong.

Let our conscience be our guide
The idea of reverence for life is very central in the Hindu religion. However, Hinduism is flexible as it offers freedom to the individual to exercise personal choices based on the dictates of his own conscience. Hinduism recognises that many decisions such as the question of abortion, should be left to personal conscience. Hence if it is found that a foetus is seriously malformed and will suffer greatly in the future, then the family may use their conscience as a guide, and may opt for an abortion. Though aborting a child just because the pregnancy was unplanned or aborting a child because it has the wrong sex would be considered highly immoral.

Legal arguments: The 1990 Act has stated that abortion can only be allowed up till the twenty-fourth week into pregnancy. There is great controversy over issues of when life is considered valuable enough to be saved, and if the foetus should be granted the same human rights as a fully-grown human being. The 'Society for the Protection of the Unborn Child' agrees with Hindu thinking, that abortion at any stage is unjust. However, the 'National Abortion Campaign' believes that the right on such issues lies with the mother, and not with society. It is her body and she should be the one to decide if she wants to keep the baby or abort it. Hinduism would suggest that the choice in such matters should be left to the individual's conscience rather than be imposed by society.

Contraception

Preventative measures for unwanted pregnancies include the use of contraceptives. Since Hindus believe that life only begins after conception, no life is harmed through contraception. Contraception does not go against the idea of the sanctity of life. Sometimes it can prevent the spread of diseases such as AIDS. However, this does not mean that Hindus promote a promiscuous lifestyle over a celibate one; contraception should not be used as a licence for lust.

Surrogacy & IVF treatment

There is nothing within Hindu teaching that would suggest that surrogacy is immoral. If for technical reasons it becomes necessary to use a surrogate mother to give birth to a child, this would be seen as a commendable personal sacrifice.

Fertility and IVF treatments would also be considered morally acceptable as they are viewed as artificial aids used to help conception.

Genetic Engineering and Cloning

Like any new discoveries in science, the initial stages of its development are fraught with danger. The use of fire in ancient times, or electricity in recent times, could have been viewed as dangerous activities carried out by mankind, but over time, we have managed to reduce the risk, and have harnessed these forces for the benefit of mankind. In the same way, Hinduism views genetic engineering in a positive light. Through genetic engineering, mankind is now trying to master and gain control over the building blocks of the body. Hinduism does not view cloning as 'playing God'. The cloning process is not viewed as creating '*new souls*'. It is simply a process of creating outer body forms for different souls to occupy. Provided this process is handled with care, Hinduism sees nothing wrong with it.

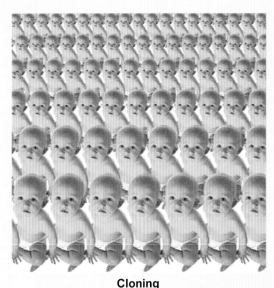

Cloning
can produce duplicate bodies but not duplicate souls

The Use of live embryos to advance medical knowledge or treatment

Research on live embryos would be strongly opposed by most Hindus, as it is regarded as conducting experiments on live human beings. The fact that the individual is at an early stage of physical development does not mean that it can be misused in this manner. Nevertheless, research done on dead embryos, or using stem cells from dead embryos, would be seen as acceptable. There is always the danger that research establishments may be tempted to allow live embryos to somehow 'die accidentally'!

Organ donation

For Hindus, the body after death is no longer significant, hence it is cremated rather than buried. Therefore, there can be no objection against organ donation in the Hindu tradition. If the organs of a deceased individual can help to save another life, then they should be donated without reservation.

Euthanasia: 'A gentle death'

1. Suicide ~ Active euthanasia

There are several categories of euthanasia. 'Active euthanasia' means 'committing suicide' or killing oneself. This is not recommended by any religion, including Hinduism. Taking one's own life is not the best way of escaping hardships in life. Hindu teachings of *karma* suggest that if the individual takes his own life in order to avoid facing serious challenges now, he is simply transferring his problems to his next life. All such problems have to be faced and resolved here and now rather than be avoided and postponed to the next life.

2. Do not prolong suffering ~ Passive euthanasia

In certain cases, it may be clearly recognised that the patient is terminally ill and has no chance of survival. In such situations, the most appropriate course of action is to make the patient as comfortable as possible. No attempt is made to cure him, as this may just prolong and cause greater suffering for the patient. Medication administered to the patient will help relieve the symptoms rather than attempt to cure him. Sometimes, the patient is placed in a hospice that allows him to die with dignity and with the least amount of suffering. The word hospice literally means a 'rest place for travellers.' Hindu teachings would agree with passive euthanasia; all present suffering is seen as past *karma* coming to fruition. All efforts to alleviate such pain would be viewed as practising *ahimsa*.

3. Help someone die? ~ Voluntary euthanasia

'Voluntary euthanasia' is the process whereby the patient, who has no hope of recovery, wishes to take his own life. This can be viewed as legalised suicide. This form of suicide is legal in Holland, and a UK organisation called 'EXIT' is attempting to make it legal in this country. In Holland, a patient can seek permission and assistance from two doctors to end his life. The doctors can assist the patient to end his life. Hindu teachings of *karma* would suggest that the patient and the doctors, by *actively* engaging in this act of killing, are clearly expressing disrespect for life and are acquiring bad *karma* in the process.

Some Hindus would argue that even though life is viewed as sacred, addressing the issue of suffering is equally important. If the patient is undergoing such severe suffering that euthanasia is the only way out, then ending life may not necessarily be seen as acquiring bad *karma*.

4. No choice but to switch off ~ Compulsory euthanasia

'Compulsory euthanasia' is the process of ending life knowingly, such as switching off a life support machine of a patient reduced to a vegetative state. The family members see no reason to keep the patient alive with artificial aids hence the patient's life is terminated. Hinduism does not see anything wrong with this. The life forces that co-ordinate the bodily functions of the patient have already disintegrated signalling that the individual soul has already departed and is no longer in the body. Hence keeping the body alive through artificial means would be seen as pointless.

5. Those special beings who discard their bodies at will

Spiritually evolved beings in the Hindu tradition sometimes discard their bodies at will. The ability they possess of giving up their bodies is a unique feature of God-realised or Self-realised individuals. It is claimed that they take birth at will and give up their bodies at will. It is recorded that *Rama*, at the end of his life discarded his body at will. It is claimed that when Vivekananda felt that he had fulfilled his task on earth he gave up his body in deep meditation.

Breadth of vision

The need to re-visit reincarnation
The ancient Greeks and some in the Judeo Christian traditions entertained ideas of reincarnation. It appears that in order to give rigour to the theology promoted by the Church fathers, the theory of reincarnation was discarded by the Church. We are now reaching a stage when the scientific evidence of reincarnation is mounting. Reincarnation combined with the law of *karma* provides 'measured rewards for measured risks' which is a far more just system than eternal rewards or eternal retribution. The idea of God inflicting eternal torment may have been useful in medieval times, but is highly objectionable in modern times.

Dignity offered to the Gay movement
Homosexuals have been made to feel like outcastes from spiritual life. The insight offered by the theory of reincarnation offers them full spiritual dignity. They are not evil in any sense; their minds and bodies have become disjointed in the process of reincarnation.

Memory Guide

Near Death Experience	Individuals who come close to death, or have been temporarily declared clinically dead, report strange experiences suggestive of life after the death of the physical body
Abortion	The killing of an unborn baby in the womb
Active Euthanasia	Committing suicide; considered immoral by most Hindus
Passive Euthanasia	The treatment of symptoms rather than terminal illness of a patient
Voluntary Euthanasia	The patient asks for assistance to terminate his life
Compulsory Euthanasia	The process of ending life by switching off a life support machine

EXTRA NOTES:

Chapter 8
HINDU ETHICS AND SOCIETY

Ethics in Hinduism ~ though these rules are binding they are *relative*
When examining codes of conduct or rules of ethics and morality in Hinduism, we have to bear in mind that, according to this religion, no law is set in stone. All rules are necessarily 'contextual.' Rules that we have inherited reflect the historic requirements of earlier societies. These rules must continue to evolve and reflect the changing circumstances, needs, and aspirations of people in modern day society. This does not mean that an ancient rule that promoted the sanctity of life suddenly becomes invalid in modern times. It simply means that the way we practise religious living must reflect the contextual needs. For example, a rule such as: 'An eye for an eye' would not be considered valid any more, otherwise, as *Gandhi* said, 'An eye for an eye and soon the whole world is blind'. In ancient times, this rule may have fulfilled an important function, but in modern times this rule would be seen as brutal and vindictive.

The ideal place to practise self-sacrifice is in the family
Hinduism emphasises the role of marriage and the maintenance of the family unit. The family unit is viewed as a convenient building block of society. The cohesive force needed to bind people together in society is harnessed through the institution of marriage and the formation of a family unit. The Hindu family unit would ideally be an extended family, which not only includes the husband, wife and children but also paternal grandparents and sometimes, paternal aunts and uncles and their children. In modern times Hindu families have also turned into 'nuclear families', which means a family with husband, wife and the children. It is the duty of the householder, (a person in the *grihastha ashrama)*, to provide financial support for his wife, his children and his parents. The householder is also expected to look after guests, neighbours and other members of his community and the society. Religious living means learning to live *for* others. A family unit only operates successfully if the family members practise self-sacrifice.

Sex is not a sin, but has to be kept under control
Sex is not considered to be sinful but it has to be kept in check otherwise it can run riot and disrupt any society. Since ancient times gender attraction has been harnessed for the good of society through the institution of marriage. This attraction then becomes the cohesive force binding two partners for life and provides a family unit for bringing up children. In contrast, unchecked sex in society results in disloyalty, promiscuous behaviour, pornography and even child molestation.

Is Sex a distraction to spiritual progress?
Religions like Hinduism are not acting as spoilsports when they suggest that sex is a major distraction to spiritual progress. The sex act identifies us with our bodies and reinforces our notion that we are 'physical beings' rather than 'spiritual beings'. That is one of the reasons why sex is discouraged for those aspiring for serious spiritual progress. The fact that the vast majority of people are incapable of living up to this high ideal does not mean that we should drag down our ideals.

Family life
An ideal setting to practise self-sacrifice

Celibacy
The highest self-discipline

Celibacy ~ An unwelcome word in modern society

Celibacy is encouraged during the student stage of life. It is compulsory for monks and those who practise *raja yoga*. Many modern Hindus consider the idea of celibacy as old-fashioned and often criticise it.

Response to some of the criticisms of Celibacy

- **"If everyone became celibate the world will come to an end".**
  Response: At any time only a few brave individuals will attempt to lead a celibate life, if they do so the world will not come to an end. There are plenty of others who will be happy to procreate on their behalf.
- **"Celibacy is unnatural".**
  Response: Electricity in the clouds is natural while electricity in wires is unnatural but offers real benefits to mankind. Mankind has always fought against nature to better himself. In the same way sexual drives harnessed through celibacy may appear 'unnatural' but produces very beneficial results.
- **"Celibacy is old fashioned while unrestrained sex is liberation".**
  Response: Since when has leading an unpromiscuous and hence more dignified life style gone out of fashion? A relationship between individuals that is based purely on sex can be viewed as dehumanising and unsatisfactory.

Is Co-habitation better than marriage?

In recent times, there has been a tendency for many couples to live together and have children without getting married. This arrangement is becoming very popular in the West, as it seems to offer greater freedom to both partners. The idea of exercising 'individuality' is considered very crucial in modern culture, though this goes against the core of religious teaching promoting 'selflessness' as opposed to 'self-centredness.' Hindu teachings do not favour the idea of cohabitation, as it suggests the inability of the couple to make a long-term commitment to each other or to the family unit. The family unit is viewed as a very necessary, stable, building block for society, and cohabitation is regarded as a threat to this arrangement. Cohabitation may also have an adverse effect on the children if it deprives them of a stable home environment. Having said this, cohabitation based on a stable long-term relationships may not be that different from a nuclear family unit. In this sense cohabitation can be seen in a positive light as a more evolved family unit.

Divorce
Exercising individuality can lead to the break-up of marriage

Infringement on 'individuality'~ is it reason enough for divorce?
Until recently, divorce was taboo among Hindus and was very rare. In fact, Hindu teachings do
not recognise divorce. Marriage is said to be for life. If for any reason, a husband abandons his
wife, he is still expected to provide for her. Attitudes and social conditions are changing, and in
recent times, divorce has become more commonplace among Hindus. Hindu teachings
emphasise that the key to maintaining a stable family unit is *personal sacrifice.* Every member
of the family must not only learn how to live *with* each other but also learn how to live *for* each
other. Every family member is expected to prioritise the needs of others over his own. The rising
number of divorces in the West reflects ever increasing self-centred attitudes. This Hindu ideal
of self-sacrifice would no doubt save many marriages from breaking down. The idea of living *for*
others arises naturally in religious teachings. Families belonging to religious communities, or
adhering to religious values, are more likely to adopt this attitude resulting in more stable
marriages.

However, there will always be some cases where the two partners are so incompatible that living
together is just impossible. In such cases, divorce can be viewed as the only practical solution
to avoid lifelong suffering for both partners and their children.

Sex and Marriage: The Hindu perspective

The fulfilment of legitimate desires, *kama,* is accepted as one of the aims of human life. Sex within marriage is the accepted norm in Hindu teachings. Sex outside marriage is not acceptable, as it suggests lack of commitment and loyalty in a relationship. Sex before marriage is also not acceptable, as youth are expected to lead a celibate life prior to marriage. A non-celibate lifestyle in the early stages of life can be a major distraction leading to disruption in education and the development of other skills.

Arranged marriages ~ a dating agency run by the parents

Hindu 'arranged marriages' are *not* 'forced marriages'. Arranged marriages involve parents searching for a compatible partner for their son or daughter. The parents first check out the social and personal backgrounds of all the suitable matches before allowing a form of dating to take place. In this way the parents provide their sons or daughters with a range of *possible* partners. The final decision is always left to the couple, marriages are not enforced against their wishes. This is seen as a very practical arrangement, as it takes into account the social compatibility of the two partners. Statistics show that a larger number of arranged marriages survive, so this method is certainly effective.

Adultery ~ don't even think about it

The Hindu attitude towards adultery can best be highlighted through the teachings of a modern Hindu saint, *Tulsidas.* He recommends following a strict code of conduct for making spiritual progress: "Be established in truth and look upon every woman apart from your wife as your mother. Then, one is guaranteed a vision of God." This is the strict injunction for Hindu men. One is not permitted to even look at any other woman with lust, let alone think of committing adultery.

Polygamy or Polyandry

Ancient Hindu law did not forbid *polygamy,* a husband having more than one wife; or for that matter *polyandry* where the wife can have more than one husband. As long as the husband was affluent enough to care and provide for all his wives, he was allowed to be polygamous. During certain periods in history, there has been an imbalance in the male to female ratio. Sometimes there were more men than women in society. In such circumstances polyandry was seen as an acceptable social practice. Hindu laws of ethics have always acknowledged that there cannot be hard and fast rules in such matters. Codes of conduct must evolve to take into account the changing needs of society. Modern Hinduism promotes monogamy. Marriage is seen as a partnership between one man and one woman for life.

Mixed Marriages

Though marriage across social, cultural or religious boundaries is not against Hindu teaching, it would object to a partner being pressurised to give up his or her own religion to accommodate this. It would also point out the added challenges faced by the couple embarking on such arrangements.

- The children may suffer, as they may feel disjointed from both social groups. They may have difficulty in relating to either group.
- Differences in religious beliefs, variation in dietary, linguistic and social habits are bound to put added pressure on the marriage. Statistics suggest a greater number of break-ups in such instances.

The role of women in Hinduism

The early Hindu scriptures of authority do not suggest the subordination or inferiority of women in any sense. It has been discovered that the primeval concept of God in India according to archaeological finds, was that of God as a mother figure. Womankind cannot be granted greater respect than being equated with God. Some of the key proponents of Hinduism in ancient and modern times have been women. Women seers or *rishikas* composed parts of the very ancient text of authority, the *Rig-Veda.* The gender that has been responsible for protecting, promoting, and nurturing the Hindu religion, in ancient and modern times, is recognised to be female.

However, some law books on Hinduism written in medieval times, such as the *Manusmriti,* do not reflect this equality for women. Such law books should be viewed as historic documents reflecting medieval practices. One law in the *Manusmriti* states that "women should obey their father in childhood, their husband in youth and their sons in old age." 5.148. However, this highly sexist dictum is redeemed to a certain extent by another law which states that "In the household where women are revered, the Gods rejoice." 3.56.

Women confined to the kitchen

During the period of the Muslim invasion of India, Hindu women were confined to the inner quarters of the home. In order to protect Hindu girls from being abducted, they were married off in their childhood, giving rise to the practice of child marriages. Such practices became the norm during the Muslim rule in India. The practice of *sati,* where many widows chose to burn themselves alive on the funeral pyre of their husbands, rather than fall into the hands of the invaders, also came into existence at this time. These brave women chose to die rather than become concubines; they are called *satis,* an honorary title meaning Goddesses who would rather die than tolerate insult. Many of these practices like child marriages, became ingrained in the Hindu tradition and had to be rooted out by contemporary Hindu reformers.

Modern Hindu women

In modern Hindu communities, a woman has as much equality and freedom as her male counterpart. She can pursue any field of activity, secular or spiritual. She can choose any career she likes, and in many cases, is also the breadwinner in the household. Being the breadwinner makes her equal to the male in every respect. This is crucial if she is not to be seen as a liability to be disposed of in marriage by paying a dowry.

The degradation of women in modern society

Hindu teachings strongly challenge the portrayal of women as sex objects in the modern secular world. To view a human being as an object contradicts the Hindu idea that we are essentially spiritual and not material beings. The use of pornographic images for commercial interests or as entertainment goes against the grain of Hindu teachings. Hindu teachings say that viewing men or women as mere objects undermines their spiritual status and degrades the whole human race.

From caste to *hereditary* caste

The religious educational bodies and the media in the West have made ample use of the 'caste system' in their portrayal of Hinduism. To gain a clear understanding of this topic, it is important that a clear distinction is made between the idea of *caste* and *hereditary caste*.

Caste

A hymn called the *Purush Sukta (Rig Veda X.90)* in the scriptures of authority, states that just as different parts of the body fulfil different functions for the benefit of the one body, people with different skills should use their diverse skills for the benefit of society as a whole, just as a person with the skills of a bricklayer should work as a bricklayer, a person with the skills of a brain-surgeon, should work as a brain surgeon, for the benefit of society. This key idea behind 'caste' was to encourage the fair division of labour in society. We now contrast this with the 'hereditary caste system'.

Hereditary Caste ~ a stick used for beating up Hinduism in the West

Hereditary caste teaches that the profession of a person is not dictated by the skills he possesses, but by birth. If a person is born into a carpenter's family he is only fit to be a carpenter. The best example of the hereditary caste system operating in the UK is the royal family. A person who is born into the royal family automatically becomes the heir to the throne. He might not be suited to this task but he is not only placed at the head of the state but is also made the head of the church! This is a prime example of hereditary caste system operating in the UK. The reason why we have offered a very English example of hereditary caste is to draw attention to the fact that hereditary caste ascribed to the Hindus is not a religious institution but a *socio-economic* one, visible in every society.

The idea of classifying people at birth as being higher or lower or only fit for certain professions has no basis in the scriptures of authority of Hinduism. The *Bhagavad Gita* states that "A person's caste is determined by the qualities he possesses" 18.41. In the next verse, it defines the qualities of a person suitable to be a *Brahmin* as, "One who exhibits self-restraint, purity, forgiveness, uprightness, and love of knowledge and belief in God." There is no mention of a *hereditary* caste system. The *Bhagavad Gita* does *not* define a *Brahmin* as 'one who happens to be born into a *Brahmin* family!' Every modern proponent of Hinduism has sharply rebuked the practice of a hereditary caste system. All of them, like Vivekananda, have condemned the hereditary caste system as an *atrocity* in the name of religion. Just as 'the Crusades' are an atrocity in the name of Christianity, but cannot and should never be promoted as Christianity, the Hindu hereditary caste system *cannot and must never* be taught as Hinduism.

Clan system ~ is not a caste system

The caste system among British Hindus has turned into a benevolent clan system. No hierarchy exists between these clans, though there is an understandable preference to marry within the same clan. No individual in any of these clans is pressurised to pursue any specific profession just because it has an association with his caste background.

Are Gay people destined for hell? ~ Hindus do not think so.

Since ancient times Hindus have accommodated gay people in their society. They were never persecuted. The theory of reincarnation offers a very interesting insight into why some people *may* be gay (See Chapter 7). The theory of reincarnation says that we, as 'souls', transmigrate into different bodies after we die. Our character accompanies us into our next life. Therefore a person who has been male for many lives would have developed 'male tendencies' in his character. If for any reason, he is then born in a female body he will feel seriously disjointed. Hence we find many gay people protesting that they feel trapped in the wrong body. This person who is now in a female body continues to be

Gay marriage
is not viewed as evil

attracted to other females, as he still possesses a male mind. This does not necessarily mean that every gay person is somehow trapped in the wrong body, but this theory offers a plausible explanation to the whole gay phenomenon. Gay people are as spiritual as the rest of the community. Hindus do not think that they are sinners destined to go to hell.

Social Issues

Let the conscience of society be our guide

In a democratic nation, the laws of the land reflect the opinion of the majority of its citizens. The laws, in this sense, reflect the conscience of society. It is expected that all Hindus will abide by the laws of the country they live in. The exception to this rule would be if an individual finds that these laws are in contradiction with the dictates of his own conscience.

Prejudice is the pre-judgement of individuals or groups, based on faulty or limited knowledge. This leads to unfair discrimination and treatment of individuals or groups. Prejudice can be based on race, class, faith, age or gender, and affects many minority groups in every society. In many cases, discrimination against particular individuals or groups occurs unconsciously, as many people are not aware of their own prejudices.

- **Racial prejudice** is the segregation of people by the colour of their skin. The cause of racial prejudice is the stereotyping and reinforcement of negative perceptions of a particular minority race. For example the stereotype that "all Asians run corner shops and live in large family groups" means that all Asians are viewed in this singular manner. The antidote to racial prejudice lies in education as it helps negate such stereotyping of ethnic groups.

- **Religious Prejudice:** There is clear evidence of religious prejudice against Hinduism in the Western media. Hinduism has received some of the worst media coverage, for example, the exposure of *naked Sadhus* at the *Kumbhamela,* or the portrayal of bizarre peripheral cults. These do not provide an insight into the central teachings of Hinduism, but present a distorted view of this religion. Similarly, misconstrued stereotypes of Hinduism have been taught in schools, portraying Hinduism as the hereditary caste system, polytheism and advocating the worship of cows!

Ageism is prejudice against people in the higher age group. Belittling old people or being discourteous to them should not be tolerated by a civilised society. In many cases old people are viewed as a financial burden. To counter this, Hindu teachings of respect, reverence and responsibility for looking after the elderly should be promoted. Hindu teachings suggest that the elderly should be cared for by their families and not by government institutions. Old people usually wish to spend their final years with their loved ones rather than in impersonal, old peoples homes.

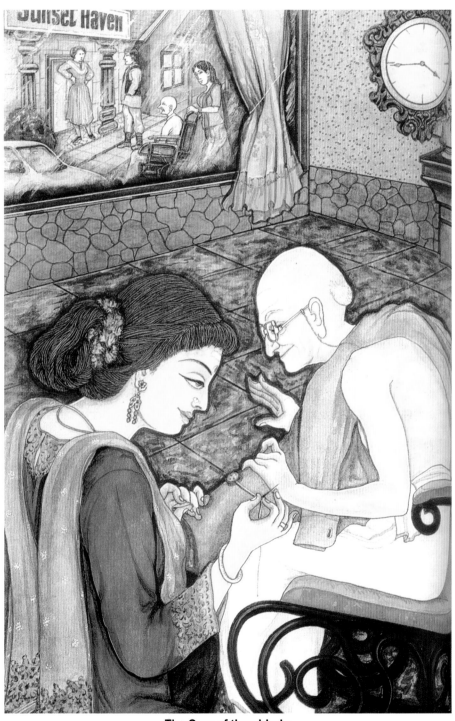

The Care of the elderly
The elderly should be looked after in their own homes

Drug abuse ~ Should we thump a TV to produce a better picture?

Hard drugs produce mind-altering experiences that can do serious harm in the long term. Hinduism offers an interesting insight into why these experiences are so addictive and disruptive. The *Yoga* system teaches that by undergoing severe mental disciplines we can enter into a state of deep meditation and gain wonderful spiritual experiences. These experiences are accompanied by unusual electrical and chemical activities in our brains. What some of these drugs manage to do is to replicate to a certain extent some of these activities in the brain resulting in mind-altering experiences.

The problem with this procedure is that we place the cart before the horse. It is the mind that should induce changes in the brain and not the other way round. So a person taking drugs is just rattling his physical system to gain a fleeting glimpse of a deeper reality. He ends up by paying a heavy price for such *free samples*. He becomes addicted to these drugs and ends up becoming seriously disoriented.

Just as thumping a TV may temporarily produce a flicker with a more focused picture, repeating such activities can only result in the complete destruction of the system. In the same manner a drug addict subjects his body and mind to severe punishment which in the long run will produce symptoms of withdrawal, depression and schizophrenia.

Drug Abuse
Short cut to spiritual experience? Guarenteed to end in disaster

Religion in the media

Media is the general term used to refer to different forms of communication. The recent revolution in communication technology has meant that the media has become a very versatile and powerful tool in the hand of mankind. Like every tool, it can be used or misused. Through satellite and internet technology we now have the power to interact with each other globally in a very immediate manner. If properly harnessed, this tool can produce great benefits for mankind. For example it can become the best tool for distributing information and education. Sharing knowledge and information globally in a cheap and convenient manner has become a reality and in principle should benefit mankind. Unfortunately if not suitably monitored, the same tool can be used to promote lower aspirations of mankind like lust and greed. The media exerts a strong influence on all of us as it can put across powerful images and ideas. Quite often we are not aware of how powerful these tools are and to what extent they can influence us.

Benefits of the media

The three key roles the media can fulfil are to inform, to educate and to entertain. If properly used they can be useful in infusing spirituality into our society. They can be used to promote values in our society and act as a suitable platform for discussing and debating moral issues. They can keep us informed about serious calamities in the world and help promote charity work. The media can be harnessed in many ways for the good of mankind but unfortunately it can also be used for promoting and enhancing the lower aspirations of mankind.

Commercial Media ~ can quickly degenerate into a vicious cycle harming society

In the name of entertainment the media can exhibit gratuitous sex and violence. It is easier to draw larger audiences by promoting such material than by promoting say, art or philosophy. The media "barons" whose main objective is to make money will no doubt choose the easier option. The funds that run the media come from advertisements. The aim of advertisements is to encourage everyone to consume more, hence everyone is encouraged to buy more than what they need, and become greedy in the process. Advertisements require huge audiences in order to become effective. Large audiences are more easily attracted to programmes that exhibit sex and violence. In this manner a vicious cycle of 'greed and lust' has been set into motion. For the moment, there is no easy way out of this dilemma; we live in secular societies that thrive on such cycles.

Evangelising in the Media

There are numerous radio and television channels on air whose aims are to convert people to their religion and make money in the process. Unfortunately one of the ploys used by these presenters is to trash other religions in order to show their own religion in a good light. Such programmes can only spread animosity and hatred between the adherents of different world religions. Most of the money collected by such evangelist channels is often misused.

The Bollywood phenomenon ~ Deceptively sweet poison fed to an unaware nation

One of the aims of the media is to entertain. Modern technology is geared to provide entertainment for the masses at a very low cost, but if there are no safety measures in place the whole enterprise can become seriously counter-productive. The Bollywood phenomenon is a classic example of the media spinning out of control and damaging the spiritual health of a nation. Critics could quite rightly argue that the vast majority of Bollywood films wallow in escapist sentimentality garnished with semi-naked girls dancing promiscuously. This process can be likened to feeding opium to the poor to keep them happy. Daily exposure to such material drains the will of the people to better themselves. Bollywood films can be described as choreographed lust set to music; such material can destroy the spiritual fabric of any nation. Satellite technology that could be usefully employed to spread useful education to help a nation stand on its feet is beaming out this crass material that is doing a great deal of harm to the spiritual health of India. The most serious challenge faced by modern Hinduism comes from Bollywood yet most Hindus are oblivious to this danger.

Sometimes so-called religious documentaries can be misleading

The funding of some so-called religious documentaries comes from suspect sources whose hidden agendas are to promote their religious bias under the guise of a documentary. Such bodies exert editorial control over the programmes and manipulate the final version to enhance their own point of view. "Compare the best of ours with the worst of others" is the hidden agenda of many of these so-called documentaries. In most cases the viewers are quite oblivious that what they are viewing is not a 'fact-based documentary' but a subtly manipulated presentation of religions.

Hinduism in the Western media

If the media is not used judiciously it can become a tool for perpetuating a biased stereotype of religion. The portrayal of Hinduism in the Western media has suffered such poor treatment. The early missionaries portrayed Hinduism as a primitive, paganistic, heathen religion; the Western media continues to portray Hinduism in the same way.

Let us examine some recent examples of the portrayal of Hinduism by the BBC:

- **Bias can sometimes be exercised through exclusion**
  Since 9/11 world leaders have been frantically trying to find a resolution to how many world religions can co-exist peacefully. The problem that has arisen in the name of religions can only be solved in the name of religion. The resolution of this issue lies firmly in the Hindu teachings of comprehensive pluralism. To our knowledge there has not been one serious programme in the West that has picked up on this. Sometimes media bias shows up through the exclusion policy it adopts. It excludes what is relevant and beneficial simply because it does not come from an *acceptable* source (i.e. an Abrahamic religion).

- **Show ours in a good light and theirs in a poor light**

  Recently a BBC Radio 4 programme examined the life of an Irish woman called Margaret Noble who became a disciple of Vivekananda and and followed him to India to devote her life to the welfare of the Indian people. She chose to work within the framework and integrity of Hinduism. The programme did not focus on the spiritual force that took her to India, but chose instead to present her as an 'Irish Terrorist' and went so far as to link her to the recent Sri Lankan suicide bombers. The programme was conveniently titled: *'Sisters of Kali.'* Contrast this presentation with the portrayal of Mother Teresa by the BBC. Mother Teresa did not work within the integrity of Hinduism but operated as a Christian missionary in India. Of course, the BBC portrays her as a saintly figure.

Sister Nivedita
The BBC dubbed her an 'Irish Terrorist' while Hindus revere her as "One who dedicated her life to the Hindu cause"

The whole Hindu nation today does not think of Margaret Noble as a terrorist but as 'Sister Nivedita' - the dedicated one. 'One who dedicated her life to the Hindu cause'. William James the Harvard academic referred to Miss Noble as a person with, "An extraordinarily fine character, a very deliberate and balanced person". Of course, Mike Thomson, the BBC reporter who presented this programme knows better.

- **Propagating instead of correcting the 'inaccurate' portrayal of Hinduism**

  A Recent BBC Radio 4 Religious programme called 'Sunday' decided to examine the issue of 'caste discrimination' operating in the UK. They were informed that just as the English class system operating in Christian England cannot be said to be Christianity; the hereditary caste system operating in India is not Hinduism. Hereditary caste does not have sanction from the texts of authority of Hinduism so the programme should make this clear. The programme did no such thing. When asked whether caste discrimination operates in the UK, the BBC was told: "The royal family is the best example of hereditary caste practised in the UK." All such comments were conveniently edited out of the programme so as to propagate the misconception that hereditary caste *is* Hinduism. This is another classic example of media bias. The BBC presenter Martin Stott had a wonderful opportunity of correcting this serious misconception parading as Hinduism but conveniently chose to perpetuate this biased image of Hinduism.

> We have singled out the BBC for criticism as this renowned institution continues to use its privileged position to propagate a very visible anti-Hindu bias. Such poor portrayals clearly suggest an Institutional Bias in operation at the BBC.

Crime and Punishment in ancient India

In ancient India, a crime was regarded as an action contrary to the general rules formulated for the good of society. The *Vedas* and *Upanishads* describe crime as an act that contradicts *dharma,* the cohesive forces in society. According to ancient Hindu law books the king or the state had to protect its citizens and punish the offenders, so that society could continue to function efficiently. If people are going to successfully carry out their *dharma*, they must be allowed to do so in safety. They must be reassured that any threats and possible dangers to themselves and their families will be dealt with. It was believed that the king must control the criminals by suitable punishment or *danda.*

The three 'R's

The modern world recognises three components to punishment, sometimes called 'the three 'R's.' The first 'R' is 'retribution' which means that the offender is made to suffer or pay for his wrongdoings. The second 'R' is 'restraint', to prevent the individual from committing further crimes. The third 'R' is 'reformation' or assisting the offender to mend his ways. These ideas are in broad agreement with Hindu teachings, however, ideas of 'retribution' translating into practice as 'a life for a life', or an eye for an eye are highly controversial. The Hindu teachings of *ahimsa* would certainly not support such ideas, even if they can be effective in reducing crime.

Capital punishment

Many nations in the world have abolished capital punishment as inhumane. In modern India, capital punishment is still in force, though rarely invoked.

- **Deterrent:** A reason offered for maintaining capital punishment is that it is the best deterrent a society can use to ensure that people do not commit murders.
- **Saves further lives:** It can be argued that by taking one life in this way, many other lives may have been saved.
- **Saves money:** It can also be claimed that keeping a dangerous person in prison for life is very costly for society, so it is better to put that person to death.

There are various reasons offered for abolishing capital punishment.

- **Miscarriage of Justice:** There is always a chance that due to some error in the judicial process, an innocent person was put to death.
- **Cold blooded:** The practice of 'a life for a life' is ancient and barbaric, not suited to a modern civilised society. A question can be asked, "How can society take a human life in cold blood?"

Can there be a just War?

Interestingly, the *Bhagavad Gita,* the scripture of authority of the Hindus was preached on a battlefield. Though wars should be avoided at all cost, sometimes they are inevitable. Society should take a stand on some key issues and if needed fight for those issues. Though Hinduism promotes the idea of *ahimsa* or non-violence it also recognises the contextual limitation of such advice. Hard and fast rules declaring what is and what is not a just war are avoided in Hinduism. The contextual nature of ever changing circumstances cannot be foreseen, hence such fixed prescriptions are avoided. The fight for Indian independence is a wonderful example of how Hinduism adopted a unique prescription for waging an unusual war.

Breadth of vision

Rules of Ethics are contextual
The fixation some religions have in literal adherence to the codes of conduct prescribed in some ancient scriptures can create serious problems for their followers. Hinduism teaches that the translation of religious ideals into codes of conduct can never be absolute, they are always contextual. It just cannot be otherwise. As mankind evolves and faces different challenges, it must be given the freedom to re-interpret how religious teachings are put into practice. The codes of conduct should be in keeping with the spirit rather than the letter of religious law.

Who has the right to re-interpret the rules of ethics?
Contemporary spiritual personalities are best suited to carry out this task. If religions are not given this flexibility then the laws they promote will become outdated and in many cases will be viewed as barbaric and unfit for the modern world.

Religions in a changing world
The exclusivist agendas promoted by many religions may have suited earlier times when religious communities had the luxury of living in isolation from each other. Now the world has become a global village and such exclusivist teachings have to be reinterpreted to suit the needs of modern multi-faith societies.

Medical research
The work done in genetic engineering, extending into research on live embryos or using stem-cells as a source of spare-parts are fresh challenges that require re-interpretation of laws of morality. Hinduism offers interesting insights into these areas. The idea of *ahimsa* or *reverence for life practised in context*, offers very mature guidelines on how to handle many such issues.

Media
The role of the media in presenting or mis-presenting religions should not be underestimated. The media is a very powerful tool that can project very strong ideas. Like any other tool it can be used or misused. If media is not carefully monitored and regulated it can easily be hi-jacked by unsavoury forces that can harm our society. How to control the media without stifling its independence is a difficult act.

Hindu values abandoned by Hindus
The strong materialistic approach to life promoted in the modern world is overwhelming India and the Hindus. The *Bollywood* phenomenon reflects the poor value system adopted by modern Hindus. They are failing to recognise the importance of their ancient value system promoting self-sacrifice, discipline, care of the destitute, celibacy etc.

Memory guide

Extended Family	Ideal Hindu family unit; includes husband, wife, children, paternal grandparents and sometimes paternal aunts and uncles and their children
Nuclear Family	Family unit including husband, wife and children
Polygamy	A husband has more than one wife
Polyandry	A wife has more than one husband
Rishika	A female *rishi*
Sati	A widow chooses to burn herself alive on the funeral pyre of her husband. The brave widows of kings who died in battle against Muslim invaders chose to die in this fashion
Tritia Prakriti	'The third gender'; refers to homosexuals in ancient India
Prejudice	A social problem that arises due to pre-judgement of individuals or groups based on partial or inaccurate information
Danda	Punishment for a crime

EXTRA NOTES:

Chapter 9
WEALTH AND POVERTY

Wealth ~ a necessity but also a danger

How can an individual make spiritual progress on an empty stomach? Without taking care of worldly needs, spiritual progress is not possible. Creating wealth is a vital requirement in every society. Hinduism recognises the importance of the creation and accumulation of wealth. One of the aims in life is *artha* meaning creating wealth. The duty of the householder, the *grihasthi,* is to earn money righteously, with which he can support his family as well as others. The second stage of life is thus considered extremely important as it provides financial support for the maintenance of the whole society (See Chapter 5: Beliefs and Values). The creation and accumulation of wealth are acceptable, as long as the wealth is then redistributed for the good of others. This is the requirement for religious living. The danger of excess wealth is that it can lead to over-indulgence and a materialistic way of life; which then hinders spiritual progress. On the other hand a poverty-stricken individual can hardly focus his mind on spiritual matters; he is too busy eking out a living to think about spiritual matters. Both too much money or too little money can be detrimental to spiritual progress.

Relationship between the rich and the poor

Religious living means learning to live *for others*. This is the conclusion of the Hindu religion. It encourages earning money for the upkeep of the family and stipulates that money should also be used for the benefit of the needy. The rich have an obligation to help the poor. Showing apathy towards the suffering of others cannot be accepted. The law of *karma* would come into operation and the fact that we ignore the suffering of others would count against us and produce unpleasant consequences for us to bear in this or future lives. The view that the poor deserve to suffer due to their own past *karma*, can result in generating bad *karma* for oneself.

Distance between theory and practice

No religion has given greater dignity to mankind than Hinduism and yet we discover that this theory is not translating into practice in modern India. How can a spiritual nation stand by and allow such scandalous inequalities between the rich and the poor to continue? The religion of a nation where the dignity of mankind is compromised, where the children are subjected to such undignified exploitation is certainly not Hinduism. The religion of modern India is *Secularism*. In their rush to embrace this Western ideal, the modern Hindus have lost out. They have lost their spiritual focus and are paying a heavy price for it.

Child Poverty
The price India is paying for abandoning its
spiritual focus in the name of secularism

Charity ~ Hindus call it Service ~*Seva*
The Attitude of serving others as living God

Why should the rich nations help the poor nations?

The practical reason why the rich nations must extend an immediate helping hand to the poor nations is because the world is now a global village. If any part of it is in distress, the rest of the world will suffer the consequences sooner or later. Just as a diseased limb, if not treated immediately can adversely affect the well being of the whole body, a remote part of the world in distress will influence the well being of the rest of the whole world. This is bound to happen; so helping others is a practical way of looking after our own interests.

The spiritual reason why we should help others is because essentially we are all expressions of the same spirit. "It is the same God shining out through so many different eyes", teaches Hinduism; so helping others is no big deal, it is just helping ourselves.

What to give?

One can offer immediate material help with food, clothes, shelter, medicine etc. This is very good, but there is another kind of charity that produces greater long- term benefits. That is *jnana-dan*, distributed knowledge. Education is the best thing one can offer. In ancient India, teachers did not charge any fees however, they subsisted on gifts. They were involved in *jnana-dan* - free distribution of knowledge. The best way of eliminating poverty is through education. Education that teaches a person to stand on his own feet and make his own way in life is the highest education.

How much to give?

Some religions make regimented rules about how much to give in charity. This is good in a way, as it ensures that everyone contributes a minimum amount towards a good cause. Some may object, as they do not like to be forced to contribute. Another question can be asked: How do we know what percentage to give in charity? That should be flexible and should be varied depending on the requirements. "Let our conscience be our guide" is perhaps the right way of judging who to give to, what to give, and how much to give.

Attitudes to charity ~ throwing crumbs at the poor?

Poor reasons for being charitable

- Some people offer money in charity as it makes them feel less guilty for leading an over-indulgent life.
- Some become charitable just because it is 'fashionable' to be charitable.
- Some become charitable as it gives them a sense of superiority.
- Some think that lending a helping hand to the poor will earn good *karma* and produce beneficial results for themselves. Such an attitude is cold and commercial.

Good reasons for being charitable

- The right attitude is to look on the poor as God Himself and serve this living God masquerading as the poor.
- The reason why we should not ignore the problems of the rest of the world is not so that the problems do not arrive at our doorstep, but because we are essentially expressions of the same divine being. Hinduism teaches that it is we alone who are suffering through all these bodies in remote parts of the world.

Contrasting attitudes to charity in Hinduism

- *Dvaita Vedanta* teaches that the individual souls are separate from God; and conveys the importance of giving through the idea of *daya,* compassion, and *dana,* charity, as ways to please God. These commandments are stipulated in the *bhakti* tradition. This approach is very similar to the one adopted by the Abrahamic traditions; they too suggest that helping others is a way to please God.

- *Advaita Vedanta* teaches that the individual soul and God are essentially the same, which gives a more logical reason why we should help others, "We are essentially the same, so when we help others we are helping ourselves." The idea of 'doing good to others' may lead to egotism, *but* the *Advaita* teaching, that charity is just 'helping ourselves', demolishes this ego sense.

Stewardship of wealth

Hinduism, like other religions, advises affluent devotees not to hoard wealth but to operate as stewards and distributors of wealth. Sri Ramakrishna teaches the man of wealth to "act in the world as a servant, look after everyone and act as if everything belongs to you, but know in your heart that nothing is yours; you are only the guardian, the servant of God." Wealth spent for the benefit of others is money well spent. There are no fixed rules regarding what to give and how much to give; one should contribute as much as one can afford. Vivekananda during his trip to the West had given a stern talk about the importance of good stewardship of money to John D. Rockefeller, who listened to his advice and set up many charitable foundations involved in philanthropic work.

John D Rockerfeller
Was influenced by Vivekananda to set up philanthropic institutions

Religiously inspired charitable work

The first generation Hindus arriving in Britain were mostly penniless and had to devote all their energies to earning enough money to survive. They were therefore not very active in charitable activities. The second and third generation Hindus, born and brought up in the UK, are now becoming more involved in charity work. At the initial stages most of their work was directed towards raising funds for disaster relief work in India. In recent times many Hindu bodies have become active in local charity work, raising funds for local hospices, medical research charities, and international aid organisations.

Work of *Seva International* in the UK

This charity run by the *Hindu Swayamsevak Sangh* does substantial work for causes in India as well as in the UK. In India they support medical camps, rehabilitation work and disaster relief programmes. In the UK they are involved in raising funds for local needs like blood donation, tree planting, or free fruit distribution in hospitals. They collect their funds through charity walks, cultural events and private donations.

Work of the *BAPS Swaminarayan* Movement in the UK

Under the inspiration of *Param Pujya Pramukh Swami Maharaj, The BAPS Swaminarayan Sanstha* has become internationally renowned socio-spiritual organisation involved in humanitarian activities through a worldwide network of 8,100 centres, 500 temples and 45,000 volunteers. This body is active in charity work in the United Kingdom. They organise many charity events to raise funds for local and international charity work. Large sums of money have been collected and sent for disaster relief work mainly in India. These bodies support many educational and healthcare programmes locally and internationally. Young and old have all contributed to various fund-raising through various projects such as sponsored walks, can-collection projects, street collections and sponsored cycling.

Charity work of the *SKLPC* and *ISSO Swaminarayan* movement

Both these organisations do substantial work in collecting and donating funds for relief work in India. They also donate funds collected through charity walks and other sponsorship activities to the local hospitals.

BAPS Swaminarayan Temple in London
The face of organised Hinduism in the West

Congregation
of ladies at the ISSO Swaminarayan Temple

Fund raising activities ~ Charity Walks

The Service of the Ramakrishna Math and Mission

Vivekananda established the Ramakrishna Math & Mission in 1897 with the aim of: "Training monks to make spiritual progress through seva, service to man". Serving the poor, the destitute and the feeble is seen as the best way of worshipping God.Vivekananda wished that "a hundred thousand men and women fired with the zeal of holiness, fortified with eternal faith in God and nerved to lion's courage by their sympathy for the poor and the fallen and the downtrodden, will go over the length and breadth of the land, preaching the gospel of salvation, the gospel of help, the gospel of raising up, the gospel of equality."

Today, the movement continues to expand and is recognised as one of the major philanthropic organisations of India. Currently it has one hundred and forty-six centres in India engaged in charitable work such as running free hospitals, educational institutes and activities for women and children. Work is also taking place in rural and tribal areas of India, raising awareness of good sanitation, agriculture, education and self-reliance.

The greater role of the Ramakrishna Order *is to revitalise the message of spirituality on the world scene.*

Swami Vivekananda emphasised the special role of India saying:

Each nation has a destiny to fulfil; each nation has a message to deliver. The mission of Inda is not political or military predominance, it is to garner all the spiritual values, to combine them and to concentrate them, to preserve them so that at a suitable moment of need flood the world with these higher aspirations - that is the sacred role of India.

The Ramakrishna Mission and Math
Service to mankind is the highest worship of God

Real reasons for world poverty

The real reasons for world poverty are not lack of food, lack of land or overpopulation. These excuses are myths. There are other, less conspicuous reasons for this crisis:

- **Lack of education:** The main cause of poverty is ignorance; it is lack of education that stops mankind from improving his destitute condition. Vivekananda believed that "real education is that which enables one to stand on his own legs." This reflects the famous adage: "give a man a fish, and he will feed himself for a day. But teach him *how* to fish, then he can feed himself for ever."

- **Greed:** Another reason for world poverty is greed. Despite the fact that three quarters of the world suffers from abject poverty, the affluent one quarter remains unconcerned and does not help redress the balance. In fact, the richer nations seem to be taking advantage of the poverty-stricken to fuel their own cravings for more wealth and power. Poor countries do not have the economic strength to counter the pressures exerted by the multinationals, andspiral into greater debt. Some attempts are being made by various organisations, like the Fair Trade enterprise to redress the balance. This encourages consumers in richer countries to only buy products that are bought at a fair price. However, more needs to be done. Unless the richer nations realise that their greed continues to fuel this inequality and take corrective measures, the problem will not be resolved.

- **Apathy:** Poverty lingers on due to apathy. We in the affluent West consider ourselves *'civilised',* but how can civilised people tolerate the fact that *thirty five thousand* people die of hunger and malnutrition every day? We surely cannot be called educated and civilised if, in our frenzy of over-indulgence, we deprive *thousands* of poor people of their basic needs for survival. The percentage of funding allocated in charity to the third world by the richer nations can best be described as a pittance.

- **Charities being run as businesses:** No doubt many world charities are doing commendable work in fighting poverty, but some of these organisations turn into business opportunities. Sometimes a very small percentage of cash raised by such charities gets through to the needy. It is progressively milked as the proceeds pass through the system. Nowadays working for a charity is a very lucrative source of income. These business charities with budgets and advertising campaigns, are a highly undignified way of helping the poor. Some Hindu charities like the *Swaminarayan organisation* and the *Ramakrishna math and mission* operate strictly on the criteria of 'no administrative costs' hence every penny offered in charity goes to the needy.

Breadth of Vision

Can we call ourselves civilised?
How can the developed countries call themselves educated and civilised when they continue to ignore the issue of horrendous poverty in the wider world? Three quarters of the world population suffer from malnutrition while one quarter suffer from over-consumption. These are symptoms of a world that is neither sane nor civilised.

Third world debt arose mainly from the strings attached to earlier aid programmes
The third world countries are unable to service interest payments on their debts let alone repay the debt. Most of these debts were created by strings attached to earlier aid programmes. It is crucial that this debt burden is lifted from the poorer nations.

A drop in the ocean
The resources offered through present Aid programmes are a drop in the ocean. It is highly unlikely that the developed nations driven by secular agendas and commercial interests would ever take this issue seriously. The resolution of this problem can only come from people who have a spiritual outlook on life. It thus becomes the duty of religious communities to work together to tackle and solve the problem of world poverty.

Insult to injury
The commercial machinery makes a mockery of the charity institutions by employing advertisements that show mankind in the most undignified and degrading state. How can commercial wizards or economists with fine-tuning skills who lack any real compassion for the poor bring about a change? Individuals motivated by spiritual zeal are more likely to resolve the issue of world poverty.

Some of the inspiring sayings of Vivekananda on serving the poor:

So long as millions live in hunger and ignorance, I hold every man a traitor, who having been educated at their expense, pay not the least heed to them.

And may I be born again and again and suffer thousands of miseries, so that I may worship the only God that exists, the only God I believe in, the sum total of all souls

The education which does not help the common mass of people to equip themselves for the struggle of life, which does not bring out the strength of character, a spirit of philanthropy - is it worth the name?

Do not search for God in obscure places, for God is there in front of you in million forms. He who loves creation is serving God.

After so much austerities I have understood this as the highest truth: God is present in every being. There is no other God besides that. He who serves all beings serves God indeed.

Memory Guide

Grihasthi	The householder; his duty is to earn money righteously, with which he can support his family as well as other citizens
Artha	Earn righteous money
Daya	Compassion
Dana	Charity
Navadha Bhakti	The nine-fold path of devotion; nine ways prescribed to attain devotion for God; promoted by *Dvaita Vedantic* philosophy
Seva	Service to mankind
Jnana dana	Charity of education

Chapter 10
'CONNECTIONS'

Religious Pluralism ~ An Interfaith ideal yet to be achieved

Religious pluralism is the recognition that all religious teachings, however different, ultimately lead to the same destination. Hindus believe that as God is infinite, there must be an infinite number of ways to reach Him. Every individual can approach God according to his own temperament and background. This idea is ingrained in Hindu thinking and can be ideally utilised to cultivate fruitful interfaith dialogue. Even the so-called 'agnostic' religions such as Buddhism and the atheistic approach of Humanism, are recognised as relevant and valid pathways in spirituality. According to Hinduism, a better definition of religion can be - 'Search for unity in diversity'. Science too, is knowingly or unknowingly searching for this unity. One Hindu hymn called the *Shiva Mahiman Stotra* reads: "As the different streams having their sources in different places all mingle their water in the sea, so O Lord, the different paths which men take through different tendencies, various though they appear, crooked or straight, all lead to Thee." To suggest that any one pathway is better than the rest is considered to be a naïve statement.

Conversion is a Perversion

Problems arise when religions make exclusivist claims or monopoly on God, insisting that theirs is the only valid pathway hence the other religions are in error! Such ideas generate missionary zeal and evangelist agendas to convert others to their faith; this is a certain recipe for religious conflict. The idea held by some religious movements that they have a God-given right to convert others has to be rectified. If one wants to convert others then one must also be open to be converted. Trying to convert others is sure to result in conflict in the name of religion. (See chapter 2)

Strife in the name of Religion

The events of September the 11th can be interpreted in two ways:
- Conflict between two exclusivist religions fighting for supremacy or
- Conflict between religious and non-religious (secular) worldviews in the guise of a hard-line religion challenging the Western materialistic lifestyle.

The comprehensive religious pluralism that the Hindus have been promoting can resolve both these issues. Pluralism allows religions to co-exist peacefully and also paves the way for a unique synthesis between the findings of modern science and spirituality that can resolve the conflict between religious and non-religious worldviews.

The World Trade Centre on '9/11'
Hinduism has a serious contribution to make in stopping such atrocities in the future

The significance of Interfaith Dialogue

Vivekananda became world famous after addressing the first ever 'Parliament of Religions' in Chicago in 1893. It is quite ironic that his address was also given on the eleventh of September. He is recognised as the first religious leader who actively promoted 'Interfaith Dialogue' on the world stage. He said that "We believe not only in universal toleration but we accept all religions as true...Sectarianism, bigotry (prejudice) and its horrible descendent, fanaticism has long possessed this beautiful earth. They have filled the earth with violence, drenched it often and often with human blood, destroyed civilisations and sent whole nations into despair." Vivekananda said that the resolution to this problem is to remove the false assumption of exclusive survival of one religion and the destruction of others. Help and not fight, assimilation and not destruction, harmony and peace and not dissension (conflict), was his message. The events of 9/11 in the year 2001 suggest that the world has not paid attention to what was said at that first ever, interfaith dialogue that took place at the first ever Parliament of Religions.

CENTRAL MUSIC HALL
COR. STATE & RANDOLPH STS
CHICAGO

Vivekananda
The first proponent of inter-faith ideals on the world stage at the
first ever Parliament of Religions in Chicago
held in 1893

In Search of broader connections

Spirituality cannot be confined to religions

Even though the word 'spirituality' is used quite frequently, very few people truly understand what it means. Some think the term reflects human values and aspirations. Some, like Keirkegaard, a Christian theologian, defines it as the human relationship to the divine. Some think it is the common subject matter of all religions, hence it forms the essential link between different religions. For this reason, some think that in a multi-faith society we should focus on spiritual rather than religious education.

Hindu idea of spirituality

The understanding of spirituality in Hinduism agrees with all such approaches, but then it goes a stage further. Hinduism says that spirituality is not only the common subject of all religions, it says that if we dig deep within ourselves, we discover that we are not the mind or the body, but essentially the *spirit*. This idea is taken a stage further; if we dig deep to discover the essential nature of the physical universe, we discover that that too, is not material but essentially *spiritual*.

Hindu teachings say that *spirit* forms the foundation or basis of absolutely everything. This means that everything we experience in terms of physical, mental, intellectual, emotional or religious realms is underpinned by the *spirit*. We can only discover the spiritual basis to everything if we are successful in going to the heart of the matter. What we discover at the heart of all monotheistic religions is spirituality personified and described as God. Hinduism does not stop here, it suggests that every disciplined human endeavour, whether it be in art or science, poetry or literature, dance or music, reveals this essential spiritual underpinning.

Awe & Wonder everywhere we look ~ this includes looking within

The most wondrous journey we can go on is the journey of self-discovery. Hinduism teaches that the most awesome thing we can ever behold is not on the outside but inside. The wonderful images we see through the Hubble telescope of far-flung galaxies; or the images we see through the electron microscopes of the tiniest building blocks of life are nothing compared to what we behold when we come face to face with our true selves. We discover and behold God. This journey of self-discovery is called *Yoga*. This requires holding the mind *still* in order to take a glimpse within.

Broader Context of Religion ~ the *Upa-Vedas*

Since very ancient times Hindus have recognised that spirituality cannot be confined to religious expressions. Hence seeing spirituality in other fields of human endeavour has been encouraged through the teachings of *Upa-Veda* or additions to the *Vedas. Ayur Veda* gives a spiritual basis to medicinal science. *Shilpa-shastra* deals with architecture of temples as well as esoteric carving of images are seen as spiritual expression through images and structures. *Gandharva Veda* sees classical music and dance as valid expressions of spirituality in the art form. The *Vedangas* or 'limbs' of the *Vedas* give prominence to linguistic and poetic compositions as expressions of spirituality.

Art is an expression of Spirituality

Art as an expression of spirituality ~ to teach and to inspire

How can we define 'beauty'? We all seem to know what 'beauty' means and what we find beautiful, but it is extremely difficult to describe precisely what we mean. Hindus believe that the reason why art forms appear very beautiful is because, unknowingly, they open up a link with our inner spiritual dimension. Hence, anything that has the power of revealing our true spiritual nature appears beautiful to us. Thus the use of art in religious imagery is strongly promoted.

Architecture to express Spirituality

- **Art in the Images of Gods and Goddesses**
  The acceptance that God can be thought of with form, *sakara,* and can be invoked in a variety of forms, is a great boon for artists and sculptors portraying God. (See Chapter 2: Concept of God). Hindus use a vast range of sculptures, paintings and images to depict God. All these colourful images, dressed in all their fineries, are a wonderful tool Hindus use to invoke spirituality. Some Hindus believe and see (*darshan*) these beautiful images as the living God; for them these images are not symbolic but are the very God they worship. Hindu philosophy sees nothing wrong with this idea, as everything, including the images, *are* essentially God.

- **Art in symbols and sculpture**
  The architecture of the Hindu temple is also seen as a religious art form. The very sight of the temple should invoke the idea that one is approaching the house of God. The elaborate artwork depicted on the walls and the *shikhara* (the central tower) of the temple, help to invoke higher aspirations of the devotees.

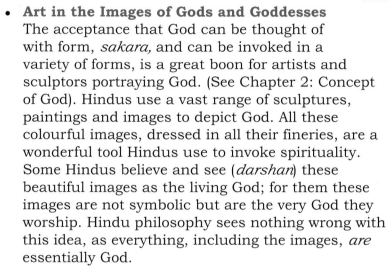
Yantra
Geometric figures that express divine order

Hindus also create geometric designs called *mandalas* and *yantras.* It is believed that certain geometric figures correspond to the sense of order and subtle inner symmetry that permeates the universe. Each *yantra* is supposed to invoke the special attributes of the deity it is associated with.

When celebrating festivals such as *Diwali,* and other religious events, many households are decorated with elaborate patterns on the walls and floors. These very colourful patterns are called *rangoli* (derived from the Sanskrit *ranga,* which means colour). Chalk, coloured sands and flour are used to create these patterns, and are used to express joy at an auspicious time of year.

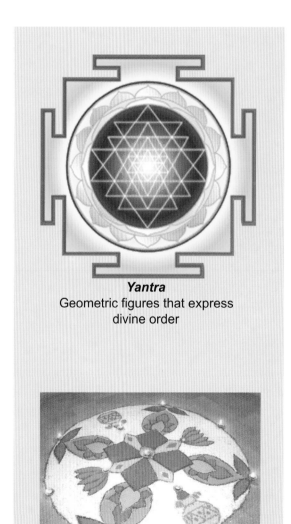
Rangoli
Spirituality is colourful

The Goddess of music

In recognition of the role of music in spirituality, Hindus venerate the Goddess *Saraswati* (See Chapter 2: Concept of God) as the 'patron of music'. By appeasing her, a devotee hopes to gain spirituality through arts and music. *Saraswati* is symbolically shown holding a *veena,* an ancient stringed instrument to emphasise the importance of music in invoking spirituality. Many musical compositions of ancient and modern periods are venerated as expressions of spirituality.

- **Scriptures set to music**

  In recognition of the role of music in religion, the hymns of one of the *Vedas,* the *Sama Veda* are set to music. The word *sama* itself means a chant or a melody, hence these scriptures present *vedic* knowledge in a musical format.

Spirituality in literature and music

- **Music in worship**

  Music is a powerful and evocative medium that stirs the soul. It is regarded as a sacred gift that can arouse devotion and love for God. Hindus commemorate God through communal singing, called *bhajans*. These are sung in homes as well as in temples, especially on special days celebrating religious festivals. Musical instruments such as drums, cymbals and a harmonium often accompany the singing of *bhajans,* and people often clap their hands to maintain the rhythm.

Poetry used to express Spirituality

Poetry is sometimes defined as an articulate use of words to express something that is beyond words. This unique feature of poetry makes it an ideal tool for expressing spirituality. Some of the subtlest philosophical ideas enunciated in the scriptures, such as the concepts of *Atman* and *Brahman*, are better expressed in poetic form than through elaborate explanations. All the hymns of the *Upanishads* are wonderful poetic expressions rather than detailed elaborations on spirituality. The flexibility offered in poetic expression is utilised to the full by such scriptures of authority. There is one down-side to this; in order to fully appreciate the poetic subtlety of such compositions one has to study and master the original language '*Sanskrit.* '

Devotional singing ~ *Bhajans*
Congregation invoking spirituality through singing

- **Poetry: Origin of the universe ~ neither existence nor non-existence**

  Hindu theology is in broad agreement with the idea of cyclic creation and destruction promoted by modern cosmology. These cycles were called *kalpa*.

  One of the most ancient hymns called the *Nasadiya Sukta RgV 10.129* (neither existence nor non-existence) describes in a most poetic manner how the universe may have come into being from a state of neither existence nor non-existence. It surmises in a philosophic manner that the cause of the universe need not be God, as He too may have come about with his creation!

Dance in Religion

The classical dance of India

- **Bharatanatyam** is one of the most ancient forms of dance that originated in the temples of India. This dance form is highly developed, as every movement, from facial expression to footwork, is infused with meaning and subtle symbolism. Dances are choreographed to relate religious stories and morals, thus offering a visual form to spirituality.

- **Communal dances**
  Garba is one of the popular forms of communal dance performed by Hindus, traditionally performed during the annual festival of *Navaratri*. The dance is performed round a central shrine of the Mother Goddess and is accompanied by music and singing. *Garba* is the adoration of God as *Shakti*, the cosmic manifestation depicted as feminine power. Worshipping God through dance in this fashion is supposed to infuse the devotees with inner strength.

Bharatanatyam
Classical dance portraying discipline and grace

Raas is another communal dance performed during the same period. Participants line up in a circle facing each other. Each participant carries wooden sticks that are struck with those of the opposite partner in rhythm to the accompanying music. *Raas* is the form of dance that was depicted in the stories of *Radha* and *Krishna* and is performed as a way of expressing and celebrating the longing of the individual soul for God.

Raas
Communal dance using sticks

Science and Spirituality
Spirituality discovered at the heart of Physics ~ the Quantum

The most exciting discovery in modern science is called 'Quantum Mechanics' in Physics. The findings of QM are more revolutionary than the findings of all previous theories of science. Two of the interesting conclusions of quantum mechanics are:

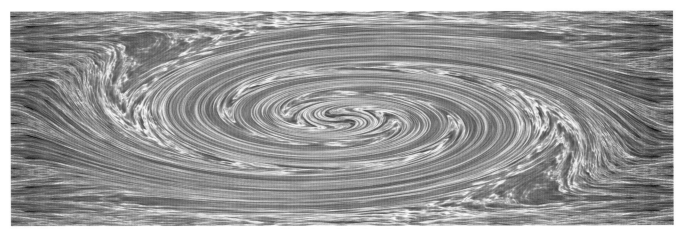

Quantum Mechanics
The primary building block of the universe is non-material

- **The world is not made of matter:** Werner Heisenberg, the founding father of this theory, concludes that the building blocks of the universe are not sticks and stones, or smaller versions of them (i.e. those famous uncuttable atoms) but something that is *non-material.* This finding of QM cannot be put aside; it cannot be altered or superseded. It is telling all *materialists* that matter is not the primary building block of the universe, but is merely a secondary phenomenon. The building blocks of the universe are not atoms but something called quantum, and the only thing we can say with certainty about quantum is that it is *non-material.* So what is the building block of the universe? The Hindus say it is the *spirit: Brahman.* Such findings discovered at the heart of modern science are in line with the teachings of Hindu philosophy.

Werner Heisenberg
Father of Quantum
Mechanics

- **Matter does not create consciousness ~ Consciousness is required for matter to come into being:** Another unusual feature to come out of QM is that the universe we observe is not an objective reality 'out there', but requires a *conscious* observer for it to come into being. This is a major issue for Physics; it does not like something spiritual like *consciousness* to enter its field and dictate terms. But without *consciousness,* the physical universe cannot come into being! So *consciousness,* which the Hindus describe as our *innermost nature* is also the essential ingredient for the physical universe to come into being. These ideas are developed in detail in the next book in this series.

One of the exciting consequences of this theory is that *materialism,* which has ruled Physics over the past few hundred years, has been dealt a deathblow. The idea that we can explain everything in terms of lumps of matter (or smaller versions of matter i.e. atoms), is now no longer valid. People of all religions can rejoice, as suddenly we have discovered what can best be described as 'spirit' shimmering at the heart of Physics.

Infinite ways to Infinity
God is infinite and there are infinite ways of portraying Infinity

God in Mathematics

Hindus see Infinity at *both* ends of the finite, and also in infinite other places
Mathematics is sometimes defined as the 'art of dealing with infinity'. Without infinity, mathematics cannot function, yet infinity is a difficult idea to grasp. Almost all religions, including Hinduism, define God as infinite. Though this may appear as mere rhetoric, Hindus insist that this statement is literally true.

When we talk of infinity in mathematics, most of us assume that it means something that is bigger than the biggest. Hindus disagree; they amend this idea by saying that 'infinite', really means *something that is not finite.* We can also have something that is smaller than the smallest (*infinitesimal*). This too, is not finite. So we discover 'infinite' when we go off the scale searching for the bigger than the biggest, and also go off the scale searching for the smaller than the smallest. Though it may appear that we are discovering 'different infinities', this is not true. We have just discovered the same infinity in different ways. Mathematics allows us to jump off the scale of 'finite' in many different ways. One of the *Upanishads*, called the *Kathopanishad,* agrees, it says "The *Atman* is smaller than the smallest, and greater than the greatest." KU1.2.20

This unique insight offers a resolution to a paradox faced by world theologians. They have been puzzling over how God can be both **transcendent** (meaning out of this world) and **immanent** (meaning the innermost nature of the world). The resolution comes in the verse of the *Kathopanishad: The same infinity* can be approached as bigger than the biggest (*transcendent*) as well as the smaller than the smallest (*immanent*). Sri Ramakrishna would add that: This infinite God can be approached not only as the *transcendent* and the *immanent* but through infinite other ways.

Breadth of vision

Promoting serious interfaith dialogue
It is difficult to see how many religions can be taught in schools in a rational form without addressing the issue of reconciling their varying truth claims. At some stage world religions have to start exploring and if needed start developing connections with each other. This process is inevitable. Hinduism has always been open to such a dialogue with other religions. The time has come for the mainstream religions to shift their stance from tolerating other religions to accepting the validity of other religions.

This should not be seen as a challenge faced by world religions but as an opportunity to dig deeper into their faiths to come up with broader insights.

Pluralism is not relativism
Many people mistakenly equate pluralism to relativism. Relativism means that there is no absolute hence 'anything goes'. Pluralism would strongly disagree. There is an absolute and the way we relate to it will always be 'relative' but then it is *strictly binding*.

Wittgenstein's legacy
In modern times there has been an attempt to keep religions and sciences separate in self-contained compartments under the guise of linguistic demarcation first promoted by Wittgenstein. It is suggested that both sciences and religions have their own separate self-consistent worldviews and as such they should be allowed to exist in their own spheres. Both these fields are considered valid *in their own way* and do not have to be reconciled. This can be described as 'relativism at its worst.' Due to this artificial demarcation, science has lost out as the deeper insights required in science to handle the major conceptual shifts taking place at its core, remain unresolved. Hinduism has a great deal to say in resolving these paradoxes. This was foreseen by the founding father of modern Physics. Werner Heisenberg (1901-1976) said something like "One cannot always distinguish between statements made by eastern metaphysics based on mystical insight and the pronouncements of modern physics based on observations, experiments and mathematical calculations." The Second book in this series *Advanced Hinduism* explores these ideas in more detail.

The broader definition of religion that encompasses findings of hard science
The Hindu religion is defined as *Dharma,* which translates as the process of looking for and harnessing the laws of nature, both external and internal, for the betterment of mankind. *Hard sciences* have already gone a long way in achieving this by exploring and harnessing the forces of the physical universe. Hinduism adds that this mastery should be extended and exercised over the inner nature of mankind as well. Without coming to terms with the inner nature of man of his mind, his intellect, and consciousness, science cannot succeed in finding the unity it is looking for. To make sense of the physical world, we are already using our mental faculties. Science for example says that we can explain the world 'in terms of *quarks*, which are purely mental constructs. We are already using our minds and intellect to come to terms with the universe we experience, so it is inevitable that we now take the next step of incorporating the inner being of man ~ consciousness, in our worldview. In a way this is being imposed on science through Quantum Mechanics.

The best ally of Spirituality is today's Science
Hindus claim that spirituality is not only the subject matter of religion but of science. The discoveries at the cutting edge of science in Physics, Biology, Cosmology, Neuroscience are all beginning to reveal a spiritual edge. These discoveries are like the distant echoes of findings of Hindu philosophy. It is by focusing on these exciting discoveries that the youth of today will be drawn to spirituality. A shift is about to take place, a shift that will take mainstream sciences into the realms of spirituality. The best way of reviving spirituality in modern times is not through the prophets of the past but through the science of today.

Evolution

Evolutionary biologists suggest that man is a highly elaborate physical being fashioned by random genetic mutations getting wound up and complex through changing environmental challenges. According to them the reason why man is special is because he is a unique piece of antique whose main objectives are to feed and breed.

Hinduism agrees with the idea of evolution but not with its conclusions. It suggests that the genetic mutations allowing evolution are not random but directed. The reason why man is important is not because he is the outcome of a unique set of genetic and environmental accidents but because he represents the fight of the spirit to manifest itself in a physical manner. Hinduism claims that we are not material beings aspiring to notions of spirituality but spiritual beings caught in a material journey.

Memory guide

Interfaith Dialogue	Dialogue between religions, if necessary agreeing to disagree
Keirkegaard	A Christian theologian who defines spirituality as a relationship between man and God
Spirituality	The subject matter of religion as well as of science
Mandalas and Yantras	Geometrical designs, which correspond to the sense of order in the universe.
Ranga	Sanskrit word for 'colour'
Rangoli	Elaborate designs traced on doorsteps at the time of *Diwali*
Bhajans	Communal devotional singing
Gandharva Veda	A Secondary *Veda* that explains the role and importance of music and dance
Sama	Literally means 'a chant' or 'melody' in Sanskrit
Sama Veda	Mostly Rig Vedic hymns set to music
Saraswati	Goddess of music and knowledge
Bharatanatyam	Ancient Hindu dance form as expression of spirituality
Garba	Communal folk dance dedicated to Goddess *Durga*; performed to invoke inner strength
Raas	Communal folk dance as depicted in the stories of *Radha* and *Krishna*
Quantum Mechanics	Forms the basis of all physical sciences, discovering that the essential constituent of the universe is *non-material*
Consciousness	The innermost nature of man
Werner Heisenberg	One of the founders of Quantum Mechanics; explains that the building blocks of the universe are essentially non-material
Infinity	Infinite and Infinitesimal are different sides of the same coin.
Transcendent	One that transcends, goes beyond the universe we experience
Immanent	One that is at the heart of everything; innermost nature of everything

EXTRA NOTES:

Resources

For Key stages 1,2,3 visit
Hinduism for Schools site:
http://www.hinduism.fsnet.co.uk

For Teachers Guide Notes
email: hindu@btinternet.com

ICT:
Links to various websites on Hinduism can be accessed through Vivekananda Centre Site:
http://www.vivekananda.co.uk/schools.htm

Bibliography & suggested further reading

- Complete Works of Swami Vivekananda on the internet can be viewed at:
  http://www.ramakrishnavivekananda.info
  Publisher: Vedanta Press ISBN: 0874811406

- Vivekananda on the Vedas by Sister Gayatriprana can be viewed at:
  http://www.vivekananda.co.uk/veda.htm

Books and artefacts

- Shri Swaminarayan Mandir (BAPS) 105-119 Brentfield Road, Neasden, London NW10 8LD, U.K.
  Tel: (++44-20) 8965 2651 Fax: (++44-20) 8965 6313
  E-mail: admin@mandir.org

- Hindu Sahitya Kendra 46 - 48 Loughborough Road, Leicester LE4 5LD
  Tel:(0116) 261 1303 Fax: (0116) 261 1931 email: info@hskonline.co.uk

- Vishwa Hindu Parishad publication with comprehensive material on Hinduism
  Explaining Hindu Dharma ISBN 0-9534354-0-7

- Himalayan Academy, Kauai's Hindu Monastery, 107 Kaholalele Road, Kapaa,
  HI 96746-9304 Fax (1) 808-822-4351 Phone: (1) 800-890-1008 USA
  http://www.himalayanacademy.com/

- Hinduism Today magazine   http://www.hindu.org/
  To subscribeE-mail: contact@hindu.org

For Literature on Vedanta

- Vedanta Press & Catalog 1946 Vedanta Pl. Hollywood, Ca 90068 USA
  http://www.vedanta.com e-mail: info@vedanta.com

- Advaita Ashrama, 5 Dehi Entally Road, Calcutta 700 014, India
  email: advaita@vsnl.com

- Sri Ramakrishna Math, Chennai 600 004, India
  http://www.sriramakrishnamath.org
  Phone : 91-44-24621110 Fax : 91-44-24934589
  Email : srkmath@vsnl.com

- Ramakrishna Vedanta Centre, Blind Lane, Bourne End, Buckinghamshire SL8 5LG
  UK Phone: (01628) 526 464 Email:
  www.vedantauk.com   vedantauk@talk21.com

For arranging school visits to a Hindu temple or Hindu monastery in the UK:

- Shri Swaminarayan Temple 105-119 Brentfield Road Neasden London NW10 8KD
  Phone 020 8965 2651 fax 0208965 6313
  www.mandir.org   admin@mandir.org

- Ramakrishna Vedanta Centre Blind Lane Bourne End, Buckinghamshire SL8 5LG
  Phone 016285 26464   www.vedantauk.com email
  vedantauk@talk21.com

**For further assistance or ordering
Hinduism for Schools book contact:**

**Vivekananda Centre London
6 Lea Gardens Wembley Middlesex HA9 7SE
Tel 020 8902 0840 email hindu@btinternet.com
http://www.vivekananda.co.uk**

Glossary

Arti Invocation ceremony or welcoming ceremony; involves waving a lamp in clockwise manner in front of the deity

Acharya Spiritual teacher who teaches by example

Advaita Vedanta Non-dualism; teaches that the individual soul and God are non-different

Ahimsa The virtue of non-violence; abstinence from harming any living being; not to hurt or harm by word, deed or thought

Antima Kriya The final rite; the cremation of the body; the final *samskara*

Artha The accumulation of wealth, one of the aims of life

Aryan Literally means 'noble one'

Arya Samaj 'Society of nobles'; a Hindu reform movement instigated by *Dayananda Saraswati* (1825-1883); believes in a formless God; brought about many social reforms; revived the ancient ritual of *havan*, worship through fire

Ashrama The four stages of life; also means a hermitage or monastery; literally means 'that which is obtained by effort'

Atman The Ultimate Reality manifesting itself as the 'I' in the individual; the real self; the silent witness; *nirguna* without attributes, *nirakara* without form; imperishable and eternal does not die with the body

Atharva Veda One of the four Vedas

Avatar 'One who descends'; God descends to earth to infuse spirituality into society; *Vishnu* is believed to incarnate ten times

Ayodhya A popular place of pilgrimage; birthplace of *Rama*; on the banks of the river *Saryu* in Utter Pradesh Northern India

Bhagavad Gita The 'Song of the Divine'; a central book of authority for Hindus; contains seven hundred verses in eighteen chapters; is a spiritual dialogue between *Krishna* and *Arjuna*; teaches renunciation and love for God in the form of *Krishna*

Bhajans Devotional singing; normally sung communally in a temple

Bhakta A devotee of God

Bhakti Strong love for God; a devotional approach to spirituality

Bhakti Yoga The way to God through devotion; involves worship and adoration of a personal form in order to build up relationship with the divine

Bharatanatyam Ancient Hindu dance form as expression of spirituality

Brahma God viewed in the role of creator of the universe; shown with four heads; holds the scriptures; is shown seated on a white lotus

Brahmacharya Celibate living; acting in a manner to reflect that everything is a manifestation of *Brahman*

Brahmacharya Ashrama The student life; involving the disciplines of celibacy and concentration on studies; respect for elders; this stage of life begins with the *upanayana* ceremony at the age of around eight; the child is introduced to the main prayer of Hinduism called the *gayatri*

Brahmachari A person who is in the Brahmacharya Ashrama; one who practises celibacy

Brahman The Ultimate Reality manifesting or projecting itself as the universe and everything; hence the Sanskrit word for the universe is *shrushti* a projection; considered to be without form and qualities, *nirakara, nirguna*

Brahmin priest A person of wisdom; person who conducts rituals

Brahmo Samaj A social reform movement started by *Ram-mohan Roy* in the nineteenth century; advocates formless God with qualities

Buddha The enlightened one; known as *Siddhartha Gautama* before attaining this state (Sixth century BC); the ninth *avatar* of *Vishnu*

Camphor Paraffin-like substance burnt during the *puja* ceremony; signifies the burning of the ego

Caste System The division of society into groups defining the division of labour; this system degenerated as it became a hereditary trait; outlawed by the government of India

Consciousness The innermost nature of every living thing

Dana Act of giving; charity

Darshan 'To catch sight of'; refers to visiting a holy place to see the image of God

Devi The female form of God

Deity The form of God being worshipped

Dharma The religion of right conduct; righteous living; that which sustains society and civilisation; the intrinsic, innermost quality of everything including the physical universe; cosmic order; (*Sanatana* means eternal; everlasting; universal)

Diwali The festival of light; an autumn festival celebrated with lamps to mark the day *Rama* returned to Ayodhya after 14 years in exile

Durga 'The inaccessible'; the Mother Goddess in the form of a warrior; holds many divine weapons for destruction of evil; is seated on a lion or a tiger, representing suppression of the ego; shown wearing a red sari

Dusshera The tenth day autumn festival honouring victory of Goddess *Durga* also commemorates the day *Rama* defeated *Ravana*

Dvaita Vedanta The dualistic form of *Vedanta*; teaches that the individual soul, the universe and God are three separate independent categories

Fasting Total or partial abstinence from food; an austerity practised for spiritual merit on certain auspicious days of the Hindu calendar

Gandhi 'Mahatma' means great soul; Gandhi used spiritual tools such as *satya*: truth, and *ahimsa*: non-violence, which won independence for India from the British rule in a non-violent manner; he called his method *satyagraha*: insistence on truth

Gandharva Veda A subsidiary *Veda* that expounds the role and importance of dance and music in religion

Ganesh The elephant-headed God; originates from *Puranic* tale; son of *Shiva* and *Parvati*; the deity of good luck and remover of obstacles; shown with a mouse as a vehicle and holding sweets to symbolise the sweet nature of the divine

Ganges (River) The most sacred river for the Hindus; flows from the *Himalayas*; a *Puranic* story implies that it washes away the sins of those who bathe in it; the ashes of the departed are often immersed in it

Garba Communal folk dance dedicated to Goddess *Durga*; performed to invoke inner strength

Gayatri The main Hindu prayer; ascribed to a sage called *Vishvamitra*; translation of the verse: 'Let us meditate on the glorious effulgence of that Supreme Being who has created the universe. May She enlighten our hearts and direct our understanding'

Grihastha Ashrama The householder stage of life; from the Sanskrit word *griham* meaning house; this stage of life provides financial support for all the other stages; teaches righteous living, looking after the family and society; begins after the marriage ceremony

Grihasthi One who is in the *Grihastha Ashrama*; a householder

Gunas Means 'threads', qualities; the universe is considered to be a composition of three qualities or *gunas*; these are *sattva*: balance, calmness, knowledge; *Rajas*: action, passion, & *tamas*: darkness, inertia, ignorance

Guru A spiritual teacher who destroys the ignorance of his student

Hanuman The monkey-faced deity of the epic *Ramayana*; a great devotee of *Rama*; the personification of strength; sometimes shown holding a mace and sometimes a mountain both symbolic of strength

Havan Ancient ritual of worshipping through fire; a relationship is built with higher beings by offering *ghee* and nine types of grains to the fire

Havan kund A pyramid shaped container in which a *Havan* is lit

Hindu A word derived from the mispronunciation of the name of the river *Sindhu*; (the word *sindhu* in Sanskrit means river or vast expanse of water)

Holi A spring festival; celebrated with coloured powders and water; also related to the *Puranic* story of *Prahalad* being saved by *Vishnu*

Incense Used in the *puja* ceremony; it burns and gives forth a sweet scent; also releases a gentle smoke that permeates the room, symbolically linked to the way that God permeates the universe

Jain From *'jina'* 'one who is victorious'; the name of the religion founded by *Mahavira* the 24th *jina*. Emphasising truth *satya* and non-violence *ahimsa*

Janamasthmi The birth date of *Krishna*

Jnana Yoga The way to God through knowledge via discrimination and dispassion

Jnani One who is knowledgeable in spiritual matters

Kali Mother Goddess in the form of the all-destroyer; she clears the slate to restart the cycle of creation; shown wearing a necklace of skulls

Kama Legitimate desires; one of the four aims of life

Karma (Law of) Law of cause and effect on personal terms; 'What you sow, is what you will reap'; we have to bear the consequences of all our actions, if not immediately then in a later life; does away with God sitting in judgement; we are responsible for our own destiny; if misunderstood can cause indifference to the suffering of others or can cause fatalistic behaviour

Karma Yoga The way to God through action; action is considered to be better than inaction. What kind of action? Selfless action; God-centred action

Karma Yogi One who has mastered the practice of *karma yoga*; a selfless actor

Krishna The eighth incarnation of *Vishnu*; the author of the *Bhagavad Gita*, the book of authority for the Hindus

Lakshmi God in a female form; the consort of *Vishnu*; the Goddess of wealth and beauty; shown wearing a red sari and offering gold coins to her devotees

Mahabharata One of the major epics of Hinduism; contains around one hundred thousand verses; is the story of the struggle of the *Pandava* brothers; dealing with issues of politics, philosophy and spirituality; ascribed to sage *Ved-vyasa*

Mandalas Perfect geometrical designs which correspond to the sense of order in the universe

Mandir A Hindu temple

Manusmriti Ancient text dealing with ethics, morality and codes of conduct written by sage *Manu*; has limited validity as it is a *smriti* text

Marga A path, a way to God; the four methods used are *Jnana*: through intellect; *karma*: through selfless action; *bhakti*: through love and devotion; *raja*: through meditation

Maya The power that makes God 'appear' as the universe

Moksha Destruction of delusion, ends cycle of rebirth; become one with God

Murti The image of God being worshipped; *pratima* meaning 'image that leads one to God

Namaste A salutation meaning: reverence to 'you as God'

Nataraja The 'Lord of the dance'; *Shiva* shown in the cosmic dance of creation; holds a drum symbolic of creation and fire, a symbol of destruction

Navaratri The festival of nine nights; in honour of the Mother Goddess

Nirvana A Buddhist term for liberation from the cycle of rebirth: *samsara*

Om The sacred symbol and sound representing God

Parvati The consort of *Shiva*; the Mother Goddess; the personification of power, *Shakti*, shown as an ordinary looking woman

Patanjali Founder of the *Yoga* school of philosophy and the practice of meditation called *Raja Yoga*

Prahlad A child devotee of *Vishnu*; connected with the festival of *Holi*

Prashad Sanctified food; food after being offered to the deity

Pratik A symbol of God; that which leads one to God

Pratima An image of God; that which leads one to God

Puja Means 'adoration'; the worship of God in the home or the temple

Puranas Legendary texts of Hinduism

Quantum Mechanics New science that says the essential nature of the universe is *non-material*

Raja Yoga The 'royal' pathway to God; way to God through meditation

Raja Yogi One who has mastered the practice of *Raja Yoga*

Raksha Bandhan A festival that celebrates the relationship between a brother and sister; the sister ties a thread round her brothers' wrist

Raas Communal folk dance as depicted in the stories of *Radha* and *Krishna*

Rama The hero of the epic the *Ramayana*, considered to be the ideal man, ideal son, ideal king and ideal personality; 7th *avatar* of *Vishnu*

Ramakrishna A recent prophet of Hinduism; highlighted the experiential unity behind various religions and sectarian movements

Ramanavami The birth date of *Rama*

Ramayana One of the two epics of Hinduism; relates the story of *Rama* and *Sita*, the ideal man and woman; written by sage *Valmiki*

Ranga The Sanskrit word for 'colour'

Rangoli Elaborate designs traced on doorsteps at the time of *Diwali*

Reincarnation A belief that the individual soul is born again and again; the cycle of rebirth that only ends when the individual attains *moksha*

Rig Veda One of the four *Vedas*

Rishi Word derived from the Sanskrit root *'drish'*

meaning 'to see'; refers to the founders of Hinduism; *rishis* claim first hand experience of God; they hold the authority in spiritual matters

Rishika A female *rishi*

Sadhu Literally means 'a good individual'; a holy man or ascetic

Sama Literally means 'a chant' or 'melody' in Sanskrit

Sama Veda Mostly Rig Vedic hymns set to music

Sacraments Rituals; outward signs of inward spiritual progress; *samskaras*; rites of passage

Sahadharmini Name given to the wife after the marriage ceremony; means 'companion for spiritual progress'

Sama Veda One of the four *Vedas*

Samsara 'Stream of existence'; the cycle of birth and death; the theory of reincarnation

Samskara Rites of passage; religious ceremonies to mark entry into different stages of life; there are sixteen main *samskaras*

Sanatana Eternal & universal; Hinduism is referred to as *Sanatana*

Sanyasa Ashrama The final stage of life as an ascetic; the individual renounces his family and accepts the whole world as his family; gives up trivial things in order to gain something far greater: God

Sanyasi 'One who renounces'; a monk; one who enters the final stage of life; can also commence when one feels strong urge to find God; the aims of *sanyasa* are personal salvation through service of mankind

Sanskrit The ancient language of India; considered to be the basis of all Indo-European languages; means 'polished'

Saptapadi The seven steps taken together during the marriage ceremony

Saraswati The Mother Goddess as the mother of all learning, art and music; shown wearing a white sari; holds a *veena* and the scriptures

Sati A widow chooses to burn herself alive on the funeral pyre of her husband. Were mostly brave widows of kings who were killed in battle against Muslim invaders, they chose to die rather than become the concubines of Muslim rulers.

Satya Sanskrit word for truth

Scripture Writing believed to be divinely inspired

Seva Service to the spiritual teacher or service to mankind

Shaivism The sect of Hindus devoted to *Shiva*

Shaivite A person who has adopted the approach to God in the form of *Shiva*

Shakti 'Energy'; depicted as the Mother Goddess

Shakta A person who approaches God in the form of Mother Goddess

Shankara 8th century philosopher and teacher who

promoted a rationale in spiritual matters

Shiva One of the forms of God in Hinduism; shown in meditation with a snake curled round his neck; is smeared in ashes; shown with three eyes; also depicted as *Nataraja*

Shradh The period of mourning for departed souls

Shruti 'That which is heard'; the books of authority for Hindus; consists of the four *Vedas*: *Rig, Sama, Yajur* and *Atharva*

Sita The wife of *Rama*; depicts patience, calmness and grace; the ideal role model for Hindu women

Smriti 'That which is remembered'; man-made books; has lesser authority to the *shrutis*; contains, philosophy, legendary tales, epics and law books

Spirituality The subject matter of religions and sciences

Swami A 'master'; refers to a holy man or monk who has mastered his senses

Swastika The symbol of auspiciousness; draws luck from the four- corners of the world; the Sanskrit root *swasti* means well-being

Tamas One of the three *gunas*; quality of laziness and inertia

Theology Systematic formulation of beliefs about God

Tilak A mark on the forehead; symbol to awaken spirituality

Tirtha A 'crossing over place'; name applied to places of pilgrimage; places to cross over to a spiritual plane; places are chosen for geographic, historic or mythological reasons

Trimurti The 'divine trinity'; refers to three prominent Hindu deities: *Brahma, Vishnu* and *Shiva*

Tritiya Prakriti Literally means 'the third gender'; title given to gay people

Upanayana One of the *samskaras*; the sacred thread ceremony; involves rites of initiation into the student life; introduction to the *gayatri*; begins a stage of celibate living

Upanishads The texts normally found in the end portion of the *Vedas* containing the philosophy of Hinduism

Vaishnavism The sect of Hindus devoted to *Vishnu*

Vaishnavite A devotee of *Vishnu*

Vanaprastha Ashrama The 'forest dweller'; the third stage in life of retirement; involves withdrawal from worldly desires; the individual spends time in prayer

Varanasi Sacred place of pilgrimage in North India, on the bank of river Ganges; considered to be the abode of Shiva; a place of learning

Veda From the Sanskrit word *vid*, meaning to know; books of knowledge; books of authority in Hinduism; divided into four texts: *Rig, Sama, Yajur, Atharva*

Vedanta The conclusion of the *Vedas*; the philosophy of contemporary Hinduism; explores the essential

nature of man, God and the universe

Vijaya Dashmi Another name for the festival of *Dusshera* (see *Dusshera*)

Vishnu God in the form of the preserver of the universe; is normally shown with four arms holding a discus, shell, mace and lotus; he is said to descend to earth ten times as *avatars* for the good of mankind

Vivah The marriage ceremony; the couple take on the responsibility of householders

Vivekananda (1863-1902). Disciple of *Ramakrishna*; a major proponent of contemporary Hinduism ; emphasises the divinity in all living beings and promotes rational approach in spirituality

Vrindavan A place of pilgrimage where *Krishna* sported as a child on the banks of the river *Jamuna* in North India; near the *Govardhana* mountain

Yajur Veda One of the four *Vedas*

Yamuna Tributary of the River *Ganges*

Yantras Perfect geometrical designs, which correspond to the sense of order in the universe

Yatra A spiritual journey; pilgrimage

Yoga 'To be one with'; a path to God through meditation or psychic control

Yogi One who has become united with God

Index